To Louise Gilbreath

♦

And the Memory of

♦

Tim Romanello

VICTORIAN REVIVAL

IN INTERIOR DESIGN

BY JIM KEMP

Simon and Schuster

◆

New York

A QUARTO BOOK

Published by Simon and Schuster
A Division of Simon & Schuster, Inc.
Simon and Schuster Building
Rockefeller Center
1230 Avenue of the Americas
New York, New York 10020

SIMON AND SCHUSTER and colophon are registered trademarks
of Simon & Schuster, Inc.

Library of Congress Cataloging in Publication Data

Kemp, Jim.
    The Victorian revival in interior design.

    Includes index.
    1. Victoriana in interior decoration. 2. Interior
decoration—History—20th century. I. Title.
NK2115.5.V53K45   1985   747.2′0498   85-2232
ISBN 0-671-53061-5

VICTORIAN REVIVAL IN INTERIOR DESIGN
was prepared and produced by
Quarto Marketing Ltd.
15 West 26th Street,
New York, New York 10010

Editors: Naomi Black and Jean Mills
Art Director/Designer: Richard Boddy
Layouts: Nancy Eising
Photo Researcher: Susan M. Duane
U.K. Photo Researcher: Sylvia Katz
Editorial Assistant: Mary Forsell

Typeset by BPE Graphics Inc.
Color separations by Hong Kong Scanner Craft Company Ltd.
Printed and bound in Hong Kong by Leefung-Asco Printers Ltd.

ACKNOWLEDGMENTS

No book is the work of a single individual, particularly one such as *Victorian Revival in Interior Design*, which brings together a rich variety of decorating ideas spanning many styles. During the preparation of the book, a number of architects and designers took time out from their own work to contribute suggestions for blending Victorian decorative arts into today's interior design schemes. Their thoughts are the core of this book, and it is to these inventive artists that I am deeply indebted.

For sharing their thoughts during the course of several interviews, I would like to thank Peter Kunz, Gary Zarr, David Mosson of DM Designs; Ira Tarter, Michael Love, and Ferne Goldberg of New York City; Frederick P. Hutchirs and Ronald Whitney-Whyte of Prisma Designs in Los Angeles; Beverly Ellsley of Westport, Connecticut; Leah Lenney of Larchmont, New York; and Robert J. Melin of Chicago.

I am also grateful for the advice offered by New Yorkers Joseph Pricci; Tom Fleming of Irvine & Fleming, Inc.; Robert Denning of Denning & Fourcade, Inc.; Jerry Van Deelen; Allen Scruggs of Scruggs-Myers & Associates; the late Tim Romanello; Edward Zajac of Zajac & Callahan, Inc.; William Diamond; Robert K. Lewis; Mario Buatta; Bob Patino and Vincent Wolf of Patino-Wolf Associates Inc.; Clifford Stanton; Gary Crane; Ronald Grimaldi of Rose Cumming, Inc.; and Dennis Roland of Mark Hampton, Inc.

Also, I appreciate the contributions offered by Lyn Peterson of Motif Designs, Mamaroneck, New York; C. Steven Swason of San Francisco; Bennett Weinstock of Judie and Bennett Weinstock Interiors, Steven Izenour of Venturi Rauch and Scott Brown, and Joan Barstow, all of Philadelphia; Walter P. Ambrose of Boston; Janet Allen of Plymouth, Massachusetts; and Jean Harwood Davidson of Princeton, New Jersey. And in New York City, Betty Sherill of McMillen, Inc,; Gloria Kaplan of Kaplan/Sandercock Associates, Inc.; Thom DeLigter; Charles Swerz; Michael Braverman; and Scott Bromley and Robin Jacobsen of Bromley-Jacobsen.

Although I relied primarily on the advice of designers and architects in preparing the text, I also consulted several merchants for information on Victorian furniture including Jim Butterworth of VanWorth Antiques in Littleton, Masachusetts, and the Johnny Tremaine Shop in Concord, Massachusetts, as well as Margot Johnson and Lewis Mittman of New York City. For her overview of Victorian color schemes, I would like to thank Margaret Walsh, executive director of the Color Association of America in New York City.

The preparation of *Victorian Revival in Interior Design* was guided by the staff of Quarto Marketing Ltd., and for their support I am most grateful. I am especially indebted to Naomi Black, managing editor, for selecting me to write the book and shepherding it through the research and editorial stages; to Susan Duane, photo researcher, who collected the beautiful photographs that give the book a zest and design sensibility that, otherwise, would be sadly lacking; and to Richard Boddy, art director, for his care in designing the book. I also appreciate the work of Sara Brzowsky and Jean Mills, who copyedited the manuscript with such thoroughness, and Nancy Eising, for her layouts.

Finally, I would like to thank Richard Horn, for suggesting me to write the book, as well as Trish Foley, Pat Shannon, Tom Clancy, and Carol Lachman for their highly developed—and often called-upon—listening skills.

C O N T E N T S

C O N T E N T S

INTRODUCTION

The next time you visit a friend who has recently redecorated, you may see more than just a rearrangement of new furniture. The changes may be subtle, like molding defining the walls, a luscious piece of antique lace draped over a table, or a fancifully carved umbrella stand gracing the foyer. Then again, the effect may be more dramatic, like a small room painted a deep burgundy instead of the white you expected.

Many of the changes bespeak another era, yet they are perfectly at ease in an otherwise 1980s interior. This is Victorian Revival, the rediscovery and blending of Victorian design and architectural details into today's room schemes.

The decorative arts of the Victorian Age are finding a comfortable home in some of the most unlikely places. A pair of commodious wicker chairs, for example, may work well on the gray industrial carpeting of a confirmed minimalist. Or a quaint, stamped-tin ceiling may enhance the visual excitement created by an eclectic mix of soft plush furniture and hard commercial fixtures. Victorian elements are influencing country, romantic, contemporary and traditional plans, as well. Interior designer Michael Love of New York City sheds some light on the reason for the success of these surprising combinations when she says, "I don't know anyone, even the most diehard modernist, who doesn't love a wicker chair."

Savor the Victorian flavor regardless of the design style you choose, but savor it in small servings. Your room arrangement should still meet the needs of a 1980s household, but even a functional design will come alive with one or two Victorian details. You may decide on a striking piece of Victorian furniture, a reproduction wallcovering or floorcovering, or you may choose to add a single architectural detail such as a cornice. Whatever you choose, avoid trying to duplicate a period Victorian room. Even if it could be done, the results would be impractical. The first rule of design, "form follows function," especially applies today. The Victorians never could have envisioned the electrical outlets, food processors, television sets, and home computers that modern design schemes must accommodate.

The Victorian Age spanned almost three quarters of the nineteenth century. Although we tend to think of the period as a single entity, styles during that time ranged from Gothic revival to the delicate, graceful Eastlake style at the end of the century. In between, a number of other styles experienced comebacks: rococo (1845–1865), Elizabethan (1840–1850), Louis XVI (1860s), Louis XV (1880–1900), Renaissance (1850–1875), not one but two Greco-Egyptian phases (1860–1870 and 1890), and Japanese (Japonisme, 1876–1885).

The Victorian Age also was a time of great social change. In earlier epochs, the wealthy dictated the dominant decorative style. The overall form, if not the details and execution, remained the same throughout the lifetime of the reigning monarch—or series of monarchs—for whom the style was named. Beginning about 1830, however, England rose on the strength of the Industrial Revolution to become the political and cultural leader of the world. In England and America, the introduction of machines had far-reaching effects. Machines eased the drudgery of daily life, enriched and empowered the middle class, and sparked a proliferation of consumer goods. Looking for a large market to purchase the abundance of products, manufacturers targeted—and ardently wooed—the burgeoning bourgeoisie. Salesmen armed with pattern books went from door to door, peddling decorative items such as porcelain. As a result, the control of taste and design passed from the wealthy into the hands of the masses.

Victorian interiors vividly illustrate these changes. In drawings, early and late Victorian rooms appeared light and airy. Furniture was delicately tapered and could easily be moved near a window for sunlight or near the fireplace for warmth. This is the feeling designers are evoking once again by blending Victorian furniture, fabrics, and accessories into today's rooms.

Mid-Victorian rooms gave the Victorian style bad press for much of the twentieth century. From a modern perspective, too much was not enough. Rooms overflowed with furniture. Windows were weighted with masses of dark, heavy velvet draperies. Floors were covered not with one rug but with layer upon layer. Tabletops and mantels seemed to groan under an assortment of lace, silver, and ceramic serving pieces for every imaginable occasion. Where our eyes see gaudy ostentation, the Victorians saw something quite different—creative clutter that represented a comfortable coziness. But even these years produced furniture and other accessories which, when used thoughtfully—and sparingly—are appropriate for rooms in the 1980s.

The road back to respectability for Victorian decorative arts was eased by a number of favorable events. As the prices of antiques from earlier periods escalated beyond the financial means of all but the grand acquisitors, small-scale collectors and many museum curators began re-exploring the Victorian era. To their surprise, they found a number of beautiful objects, which were promptly purchased and incorporated into public and private collections. As Victorian objects began to be exhibited in houses and museums, the public gained a new awareness of them, leading to acceptance—and with a growing understanding—to appreciation. Manufacturers of home-furnishings products helped, too, by initiating reproduction programs that increased the style's visibility and availability. Then, in 1970, the Metropolitan Museum of Art in New York City legitimated Victorian decorative arts by exhibiting some of its finest examples to rave reviews.

Fueled by other factors, the aesthetic and financial appreciation of Victoriana continues today. With the influence of modernism lessening, people are looking for a new style. Industrial minimalism and postmodernism have been presented as alternatives, but their impact has been minimal. In times of doubt, designers tend to look back in time for answers. Borrowing from the varied Victorian Age seems somehow appropriate in this era of decorative eclecticism. Hand in hand with the waning of modernism is a revolt against its credo, "Ornament is crime." Now, a sense of decoration, whether it be architectural ornamentation, lavish fabrics, or prominently displayed "collectibles," is preferable.

Equally important is a renewed desire for natural materials in our living environments. Victorian objects supply this. While much from the era was machine-made in mass quantities, the materials themselves were quite often superb. Furniture was

The bibelots of the Victorian Age have found a new home in the interior design schemes of the 1980s. Architects are rediscovering crown molding and other building elements. Meanwhile, decorators are adding Victorian-inspired fabrics and wallcoverings as well as nineteenth-century furniture, sewing techniques, and accessories. Here is a sample of what the excitement is all about: old picture frames, lamps, and an imposing sideboard.

constructed with beautiful mahogany and oak instead of particle board. Textiles were woven with natural fibers. And in the early part of the period, fabrics were colored with soft dyes derived from plants, not chemicals.

Fortunately, the Victorian Age is recent enough, and its output so prodigious, that acquiring decorative arts of the period presents no problem. In exploring Victoriana on your own, you may want to consult *The Designer's Resource*, a 5,000-page catalog of manufacturers of reproduction details used by many architects and designers. The entire catalog consists of twelve volumes, each covering a specific type of detail such as plaster ornaments and columns. It sells for $116.50 from the Designer's Resource of Los Angeles. The volumes can be purchased separately. Another excellent source is *The Old House Journal Buyer's Guide*, which also lists sources for reproduction architectural elements, lighting fixtures, and more. The mailing address is in Brooklyn (see "Useful Addresses").

Antiques shops, estate sales, and auctions are other great places for finding genuine Victorian pieces. Scan newspapers for announcements of offerings by private collectors, or shop the numerous emporiums that have sprung up in recent years dealing in architectural elements. Many of these emporiums stock windows, doors, moldings, paneling, and ornaments from old buildings—often Victorian—that are slated for demolition.

To help sort out the wide selection of Victoriana available and to skillfully blend those elements into your home, you may find it worthwhile to hire an interior designer. Thoroughly trained in contemporary space-planning techniques, these professionals are adept at coordinating furnishings, colors and fabrics. (For suggestions on selecting and collaborating with an interior designer, see "How to Work with a Designer.")

Victorian Revival in Interior Design brings to your attention the many fine objects of the Victorian Age that deserve recognition and celebration. It takes you on a tour of a typical house today, beginning with the foyer and progressing through the kitchen, the dining room, and the living room to the bathroom, the bedroom, and special places like the study and media room, and even to the outdoors. As it progresses from room to room, the book illustrates specifically how Victorian elements can be artfully blended into today's most popular design schemes. Some decorating ideas suggested are applicable to more than one room. At the back of the book is a representative listing of manufacturers, retail outlets, and mail-order sources selling authentic and reproduction Victorian articles. The rooms and the Victorian furnishings that grace them are functional for today and represent lasting beauty for tomorrow. In so doing, the following pages honor the best of the Victorian revival.

CHAPTER ONE

THE HALLWAY

♦ ♦ ♦ ♦ ♦

The foyer is a paradox. It is the least—and yet most—important area in the house. In one respect, the foyer simply serves to get you from the front door to the living room. It is so unimportant, in fact, that many modern houses and apartments don't have a foyer.

But the Victorians recognized the foyer as an eminently practical space of great value. It supplies storage for overcoats, raincoats, boots, scarves, and other outdoor gear. It is also the place where we drop our keys, hats, and loose change. At the same time, the foyer or entrance hallway sets the tone for the entire house and creates a lasting first impression for guests. Designer Ronald Grimaldi says, "When you open the front door, you have to feel welcome. If you get that feeling at the very beginning, you tend to dismiss other aspects of the house that may not be so nice."

The Victorians took great care in furnishing foyers and hallways and, in effect, treated larger ones as auxiliary living spaces. Almost always, the foyer would have a hall tree for hanging coats and hats, a mirror for checking appearances, and a table with chairs for quiet conversation or occasional teas.

Today's hallways may be too small for entertaining, but they can still reflect a Victorian flair, be practical, and extend a warm welcome to all.

The owners of this beautifully restored house took a cue from the Victorians and are using a large stair landing as living space. Simple furnishings highlight the etched-glass pocket door. Note how the owners have matched the plants to the etching.

A number of Victorian elements are especially appropriate for today's foyers and halls. They include:

- ◆ Coffered ceiling
- ◆ Sponged walls
- ◆ Oriental rugs
- ◆ Wicker settee
- ◆ Hall tree
- ◆ Wood-framed mirror
- ◆ Brass wall sconces
- ◆ Thick crown molding

Many of these elements are compatible with popular design schemes today. The Victorian effect may be created in several ways—by incorporating only one, all, or a combination of the elements mentioned above. For some specific ideas, each design scheme is discussed individually below.

Langdon Clay

An ornate mirror at the top of the stairs increases the illusion of spaciousness and provides the owners of this house with an opportunity to check their appearance before descending the stairs to meet their guests.

TRADITIONAL

A traditionally designed room often brings to mind a richness of Georgian, Queen Anne, or Chippendale furniture, glazed chintz upholstery and draperies in regency stripes, an abundance of throw pillows, and a large Oriental carpet. The effect is stately reassurance—of a room that will always be in style, regardless of the latest vogue design.

Picture this scene enlivened with a Victorian aura. It may come from a large Victorian console with a painted finish in a floral motif. Or from a single mahogany or rosewood chair highlighted with carved rococo motifs. A foyer also welcomes a distinctly Victorian touch such as a papier-mâché chair with ivory inlays on the arms and legs. Papier-mâché furniture is widely available in better antique shops. If you can't find a piece to your liking, consider having one made by a papier-mâché artist such as Joe Turner in Los Angeles.

If fabricated in the true Victorian manner, the chair or other piece of furniture will consist entirely of papier-mâché, a surprisingly sturdy medium that can support the weight of an average-sized adult male. It's cheaper to buy a prefabricated chair frame over which the papier-mâché is layered like a veneer. A pale paint—pink, green, or blue—can be added to the wet papier-mâché mixture to give the finished chair a slight tinge of color. You may want to try to papier-mâché a console table bought at a local unfinished-furniture outlet too.

Another seating option is an upholstered chair or settee. For a touch of modern Victoriana, cover it with a chintz in the traditional manner but pick a pattern of exquisite Victorian paisley in celadon green, pale blue, or gold on a subdued background of black or navy blue. For authenticity, embellish the upholstery with frankly extravagant four-inch-long fringe in a color matching the paisley design. For maximum flexibility, and for a fresh look all year-round, go with fringed slipcovers in different colors that can be easily switched as the seasons change. Carry the fabric pattern through to other areas and make lamp shades. If the foyer has a window, the same pattern can be used for draperies.

Because chintz is part and parcel of the traditional design scheme, it is a perfect wallcovering and adds a softness to the foyer, particularly when the color choice is in the spectrum of paler greens and blues on an ivory background. For a more dramatic effect, choose a design in a late Victorian crimson or scarlet on a dark burgundy or even black background.

To keep this decorative technique from overpowering the room, most designers suggest upholstering only one wall. The other three can be painted in one of the colors from either the pattern or the ground.

Furnished with a small table beneath a shuttered window, this traditionally styled stair landing at left doubles as a relaxing spot to read or take tea. Ornate woodwork is highlighted with a contrast-ing paint color so that it stands out from the plain walls.

The Victorians' obsession with detailing is amply revealed in their carpeting. Gar-lands surround an asymmetrical pattern of flowers and leaves that starkly con-trast with a dark ground in the sample below. Detailing can be casual, too, as in the photo at the bottom in which a nineteenth-century hall tree holds a bevy of hats for all seasons.

Langdon Clay

Evocative of eighteenth-century classical design, a swirl of stairs leads down to a checkerboard-patterned tile floor in the foyer illustrated on the opposite page.

An Oriental runner creates an interesting interplay of pattern and texture on this stairway. The aura of elegance is heightened by fringe on either side of the floorcovering.

The same strategy can be employed with wallpaper. Limit a strong pattern—a floral, for example—to one wall, with a complementary, solid paint color applied to the others. If you want paper on all four walls, try a subdued floral or geometric pattern that has been adapted from a Victorian motif.

Both fabrics and wallpapers in Victorian colors and designs have come onto the market in recent years, thanks to the growing movement to restore and preserve old houses. Fortunately, many of these products are sold at retail. Usually, they are carried by larger department stores such as Bloomingdale's, Macy's, and Gimbels, as well as by many neighborhood paint stores. Among the most prolific manufacturers of historic fabrics and wallpapers are Scalamandre Silks, Inc., Brunschwig & Fils, and Schumacher and its subsidiary Waverly Fabrics. Cowtan & Tout sells reproductions of William Morris fabrics that are hand-printed with the same blocks that have been in use since the mid-nineteenth century.

In planning the treatment of surfaces, don't neglect the floors. A nineteenth-century Oriental rug is visually smashing, as time and wear have probably given it an excellent patina. However, because authentic period pieces are now highly prized, and thus, valuable, they properly belong in a vault rather than on the floor. For that reason, why not consider a modern reproduction or Wilton-Axminster-design carpet? Many of these are available in retail department and specialty rug stores and from designer and architect trade sources including Stark Carpet Corp. A four-by-six rug is a suitable size for a small vestibule-type foyer.

Because the foyer is a high-traffic area with plenty of wear and tear on the floor, you may want to dispense with a rug entirely. An

Sam Sweezy

The spiral of stairs shown above leads down to this lovely foyer furnished with an exuberantly designed long-case clock, a classically inspired side table, and a serpentine-shaped settee. The detail in this scheme appears along the edges of the stair carpeting.

A modern runner offers stark visual contrast with the elaborate woodwork and sleek floor in this robust foyer.

Peter Paige

Richard S. Mandelkorn

The filigree of the Victorian Age is aptly illustrated in this entry. A colorful stained-glass insert in the front door reflects a Victorian Renaissance feeling. It is surrounded by architecturally inspired colorless stained glass in an intriguing and highly detailed set of patterns.

Stained glass takes on an entirely different atmosphere in this doorway. Colorful medallions are emphasized by a monochromatic field creating an intricate array of patterns.

Neil Lorimer/EWA

excellent option, keeping with the Victorian style, is to paint a wood floor with a border design. Protected by several coats of polyurethane, a painted finish will last for years with only an occasional damp mopping.

A traditional foyer is also an excellent setting to highlight a striking Victorian accessory. Placed atop a pedestal, a large jardiniere overflowing with a Boston fern transcends the term "accessory" by becoming the focal point of the entire space. Another idea many designers recommend is to make the foyer an exhibit area for prized collections. These can range from small items, such as seashells, arranged attractively under a brass or porcelain lamp, to nineteenth-century paintings, prints, or posters. A variation is to surround a favorite piece of contemporary art with a compatible nineteenth-century frame. You can find frames such as these at antiques stores and even some junk shops.

Adding period-style architectural ornamentation can produce subtle and often unnoticed effects that visually unify the foyer. A chair rail along the wall not only protects it from furniture scratches, but also divides the wall into two halves, allowing you to apply contrasting wallpapers or colors above and below. Painted wainscoting and ceiling beams are two methods of adding architectural interest and a Victorian flavor to a traditional foyer, particularly in modern apartments and houses that usually are devoid of such amenities.

CONTEMPORARY

Though you might think that a contemporary design scheme could not absorb Victorian details and endure, there are some striking juxtapositions that can be created. A reproduction Victorian chair with ornate carving can simply be upholstered in a modern fabric. Or the reverse is equally eye-catching—a modern chair covered with a gaudy print with pattern-over-pattern floral motifs.

One of the most visually interesting Victorian touches for a contemporary scheme is a wall upholstered in black horsehair fabric. Available through Stroheim & Romann, a designer resource, the fabric imparts a look that is sleek, hard, and soft all at once. If covering a wall with the fabric seems to be too much, use it to upholster an antique or reproduction chair.

On a modern black slate or bluestone floor, indulge in a small Oriental rug. Or give your floor a look that is both old and new at the same time—cover it with wall-to-wall carpeting. This sort of carpeting looked much different in the nineteenth century because of the narrower loom widths, but it was frequently used in city houses.

An otherwise contemporary foyer subtly hints of Victoriana with a stained-glass window, while in the adjacent living area, the floor is given added visual emphasis with an Oriental rug.

In this renovated house, contemporary skylights overlook a refurbished stairway decorated with nineteenth-century-inspired wallpaper, wainscoting, and molding painted a contrasting color.

If you want easy-care floors—and who doesn't these days—the solution in the Victorian vein is ceramic tile. Small, one-inch floor tiles with six sides, commonly seen in bathrooms of old houses, can be transplanted to almost any room, including the foyer. Instead of copying the antiseptic, solid white tile floors put down in the 1920's, hark back to the Victorians' style that consisted of designs, many of which were extremely elaborate, made by blending different shades of the same color. The pattern could be as simple as alternating black and white tiles, or as elaborate as "key" designs similar to those found on modern Chinese rugs.

Various shades of a Victorian color like celadon or emerald green can be combined in the more complex designs.

Lighting in a contemporary setting is usually thought of only in terms of track fixtures hung from the ceiling. Far more visually interesting—and true to the spirit of the Victorians—would be to use a simple brass chandelier with sedate but elegant frosted-glass globes. A crystal chandelier adds a sparkle that becomes even brighter when the light is reflected by a mirror placed on a nearby wall. In this case, light beiges, tans, and ivory are appropriate for the walls, as are sophisticated dark green and black—colors that are in vogue again. Avoid the deep burgundies and winelike reds of the High Victorian Age, as these evoke too heavy an atmosphere.

Equally exciting in a contemporary scheme are Victorian accessories. The range from which to choose is great. Wax or paper flowers, or flower bouquets made of beadwork and seashells placed inside a protective glass dome create a quaint and welcoming atmosphere in the foyer. For a touch of drama, drape a Victorian cashmere shawl in a paisley design weighted down with fringe over a small table.

ROMANTIC

Many of the Victorian elements that blend well into a traditional design scheme are equally at home in the romantic decor so popular today. The key to a successful romantic scheme is restrained abundance. Here is the perfect opportunity to indulge in fabric wallcoverings, draperies, draped tables, plush—and lush—upholstery, lamp shades, overstuffed furniture, intricately carved tables, contemporary parsons tables, classically inspired candlesticks, and plenty of accessories such as throw pillows, knick knacks, photographs, and thick, luxurious carpets in vivid colors.

In a foyer that radiates the feeling of romanticism, furniture can be playful as well as practical. If space permits, a chaise longue strikes exactly the right note. For a light and airy spirit, however, choose pale-colored upholstery: a cotton chintz in a quiet geometric pattern is appropriate, or a solid light pink or yellow embellished with fringe of the same color. Satiny white, black, or navy will give the furniture a dramatic touch, especially in a room with pale walls.

The chaise frame, if simple, exposed wood, should be left natural. Or you may want to pickle it by applying white paint, then wiping the wood surface with a soft cloth. The amount of white you leave determines the extent of the pickling. You can do this process yourself or pay a local painter. A subtle alternative is to paint the frame a solid light color in either a flat latex or a high-gloss enamel for a touch of sleek glamour.

If you don't have much room in the foyer, the simplest way to add a Victorian touch is to drape a round table with glazed chintz fabric that reaches to the floor. Choose a romantic hue, perhaps a pale pink ground with a design of large pink roses and lacy green leaves such as Barbara Cartland's "Ribbons and Roses" pattern from her *Decorating With Love* collection.

Add a light-grained hall tree from the late Victorian period, but instead of leaving it bare until friends arrive, bedeck it with a collection of straw hats decorated with pretty ribbons in light pastel colors.

In this romantically imbued foyer, floral-patterned wallpaper and woodwork painted varying colors create a sense of detailing and abundance inherent in this design style. An intricately patterned Oriental runner and rug enhance the feeling. To draw attention to the various elements, the ceiling has been left simple. Note, too, how the door and window molding complement the scene.

If you have sufficient room, a small-scale chair such as a tiny ballroom chair is also practical. It can be treated in several ways to bring out the feeling of Victorian romance. A wood chair can be draped with raw linen that is secured in place with tiebacks. If the chair is upholstered, again consider glazed chintz with a light background and pastel pattern. You might make several sets of slipcovers in the same pattern but in various colorways. Manufacturers such as Scalamandre Silks and Brunschwig & Fils usually offer the same pattern in four or more different combinations of color to meet market demands. Choose a single color that

Graham Henderson/EWA

One visually smashing piece of furniture can set the proper tone in a romantic setting. Here, the owner has furnished the entry with a wrought-iron hall tree garnished with a straw hat and bag. While setting the appropriate mood, this simple approach to decorating leaves the foyer free of unnecessary clutter and enables the owner and her guests to move through the space with ease.

appears in all of the colorways for draperies and tiebacks, or repeat the pattern of the fabric draped over the table in the drapery liner. This gives a tailored, coordinated look that demonstrates your attention to detail.

Or, apply that wonderful Victorian standby—fringe—along the edges of the draperies, but keep it short, about one or two inches long. Fringe is available in many sewing shops in a variety of colors, from solid Victorian gold for a feeling of lavishness to light-toned greens, blues, and pinks.

As is appropriate for a more traditional design scheme, an Oriental rug is a beautiful addition to a room that evokes romance and a certain planned informality. A modern reproduction in a light Victorian floral pattern or a similarly colored dhurrie rug immediately establishes the proper romantic tone.

This same sort of practical-but-decorative approach is desirable in accessories. A woven basket atop a hall table is a convenient place to drop your keys. Framed pieces of antique lace can preserve household memorabilia and provide interesting wall hangings at the same time. Scour the secondhand junk and antiques stores to uncover an umbrella stand. The Victorians made many beautiful stands in both wood and metal that can be incorporated easily into a romantic scheme. The designs range from the utilitarian to the exotic—carved bears, seals, and birds. Besides adding a touch of texture and whimsy, playful yet practical accessories give the romantically imbued foyer a sense of humor that is a part of every great interior.

MINIMAL

Of course, the romantic look will leave the orthodox minimalist speechless. The minimalist, however, can still be vulnerable to the appeal of Victorian touches. For many people, even some who like the drama or spareness of minimalism, the emphasis on platforms, gray industrial carpeting, and white walls is entirely too cold and severe. Add a Victorian detail, and the look is softened dramatically. There are two keys to involving a Victorian flavor in a minimalist's design scheme. The first is to rely on natural materials that will play off the industrial elements inherent in the minimalist approach. Lightly scaled furniture and pale objects stand in contradiction to the dark gray and hard metals, creating a design tension that adds to the visual interest and appeal of the room. The second rule is to honor the spirit of minimalism and carefully edit your additions.

For example, consider the difference a single white wicker chair will make in a minimalist foyer. With solid gray back and seat cushions to match the carpeting, the white wicker frame takes on an air of sculpture. Yet the intertwining weave brings a sense of embellishment to the stark space. A more subtle combination of

Phillip Ennis

Because of their narrow width and, often, great length, hallways are difficult spaces to decorate. To leave the passageway uncluttered, the owner of this house concentrated on the walls. They are painted freehand style with flowers and drooping garlands on a sponge-painted surface, creating a textured look. A plain rug softens footsteps past the bedrooms.

Bill Rothchild

Painted finishes in eighteenth- and nineteenth-century designs enliven this hallway that connects a master bedroom and bath. Wreaths of garlands draw attention to the exquisite woodwork of the closet doors and built-in bureau. The aura of elegance is achieved through simple means, making an otherwise dull space assume a life of its own.

Stained glass, straw hats, an ornate jardiniere, and intricate woodwork combine with the checkerboard-patterned tile floor to create a highly eclectic feeling.

Two methods of achieving Victorian elegance: Long-case clocks set the tone in an austere hallway, below, while a complex tile pattern on the floor provides the same feeling in another hallway setting, right. Each illustrates how versatile Victorian design elements can be and how they can easily be incorporated into houses and apartments today.

Jeffrey Weiss

Morley Von Sternberg

minimal and Victorian sensibilities may be as simple as a low contemporary bench with soft glove leather upholstery that has been tufted in the Victorian manner.

Blending Victorian accessories into a minimalist design scheme requires great thought and careful selection. A number of designers suggest adding a mirror in an exuberantly carved Victorian frame that has been stripped, then pickled or bleached. Another suggestion is a solitary painting from the nineteenth century, or a large porcelain vase brimming with bright red roses.

ECLECTIC

To succeed, the eclectic design scheme must be a deft blend of opposites—furniture from different periods and in different styles as well as design elements that are hard and soft, old and new, shiny and textured, industrial and residential, in soft and brilliant colors. Because this sense of contradiction is the heart of eclecticism, the elements that mesh best with the light Victorian pieces are contemporary, hard, and industrial in a range of colors.

A round-back chair reminiscent of the Victorian rococo pieces looks great, as does an antique or reproduction hunt table in light-grained oak. A more casual atmosphere is achieved by replacing the rococo chair with one made of wicker. This type of seating can be painted white, with back and seat cushions upholstered in a paisley design fabric. Or, the chair can be painted a pale pastel with matching pillows added. For a truly eclectic look in a foyer, paint the chair a zestful high-gloss black with intense red or shocking pink cushions.

Contemporary white lacquer furniture gives a foyer painted in a light tan or beige a look of elegance, especially if the seating units are upholstered in that most Victorian of fabrics—velvet—in a contemporary pale color.

If the foyer is small, you may want to borrow from the romantic scheme and place a small table skirted to the floor with a light green and pale pink fabric enlivened with a pattern of berries.

One of the most useful and eye-riveting pieces of furniture to place in the foyer is a large armoirelike chest (see "The Living Room" for additional details). Genuine armoires from the late

A swath of paint draws attention to a stairway and contrasts nicely with the knotty pine flooring in the foyer, right. With stenciling the country stairway on the far right becomes the center of attention; the design is a variation of the wallpaper border in the foyer of the house. The interplay of pattern remains light and airy, evocative of country-style decorating, and contrasts nicely with a dark-stained chest.

nineteenth century abound, as do many fine reproductions. Stripped to the natural wood grain, such a chest becomes a focal point of the space, regardless of the color scheme, which, in this case, might well be a mid-Victorian navy blue or emerald green. If left natural, the chest can be embellished with a floral or country landscape scene in the trompe l'oeil fashion. Besides being the center of visual attention, the chest provides plenty of storage space for coats and gloves and even for spillover books from the study—all concealed from view.

For additional contrast, place white ceramic tile on the floor and cover the ceiling with stamped tin painted a pale green. The tin can be found at a shop selling recycled architectural elements or ordered from AA Abbingdon Affiliates.

To enliven a wood floor that has been bleached, place a contrasting dark-green metal column in a relatively uncrowded corner. New lightweight aluminum columns in classical shapes are available through Moultrie Manufacturing Company.

More than any other design scheme, the eclectic room can absorb—and come visually alive—by adding a variety of textures. Instead of limiting yourself to an Oriental rug as a floorcovering, do what many of the Victorians did and lay down sisal matting.

In most eclectic interiors, color is the thread that unifies the many disparate elements. Choose a pale Victorian rosy pink, for example, and apply it uniformly to all woodwork. Then, select a textured rug, perhaps a brightly colored kilim or a modern reproduction that repeats the color in the pattern. Other colors in the foyer—for upholstery, exposed frames of furniture, and accessories—can be left natural for contrast. Light Victorian

rian flourishes and other elaborate decoration. For pure funk, search secondhand shops for an old wood croquet set and place it in the entry as an obvious prop.

COUNTRY

At the heart of country decor is a pleasing blend of clean-lined, light-toned furniture, bright colors, and natural materials including woven baskets and pottery for accessories. Generally, to reinforce the casual atmosphere, furniture groupings should be composed of unmatched pieces. They need to be coordinated, however, by being the same scale, having the same finish, or being upholstered in the same materials.

The secret to adding Victorian touches to a country-style foyer is to choose late nineteenth-century furniture with rectilinear lines such as golden oak bookcases, a small-scale marble-topped table or a single wood bench. Beneath a mirror, place a chest for extra storage. The chest can be borrowed from the Victorian cottage style, which is enjoying a great revival in home furnishings. These pieces were made of pine or oak and painted in pastel colors—celadon green or mauvelike rose—with designs of cabbage roses or fanciful birds. These are sold at country auctions, secondhand shops, and, sometimes, even junk stores.

By all means, stay away from the dark mahogany pieces and those with more florid lines and carving. They are entirely too formal for the relaxed feeling you want to evoke.

Wood floors are particularly apt for both a country and Victorian foyer. Because rural Victorian houses lacked the panache of their big-city counterparts, their owners often painted the floors in jewel tones such as deep red or navy blue. A contemporary adaptation of this approach is to paint the floor biege or tan. Or, the floor can be left natural and the traffic area carpeted with a pink runner, which, surprisingly, is still found in many period Victorian country houses. An Oriental rug works well here, too.

Walls in a Victorian country vein are best left a light ivory or pale pastel. You can reinforce a country motif with a small-patterned wallpaper similar to the Laura Ashley prints. Other wallpapers fitting for the country style are the flower sprigs of the "Young Bunch" collection from Benchmark and "Fleurettes de Diana" by Huntington House.

The Victorians also covered their walls with embossed wallpapers. A line by Focal Point consists of white-on-white patterns that can be left as they are or painted another solid color. Again, feel free to borrow from the cottage look. The most common wallpaper element in this genre is a large floral pattern of cabbage roses.

Accessories with a Victorian air go well in a country foyer. Consider an antique hat rack made of cast iron painted white or an

colors such as pale blue, green, ivory, and yellow will work equally well, as long as they are combined with contrasting colors creating the contradiction inherent in the eclectic approach.

This setting welcomes accessories from varying styles. Consider that vintage Victorian greenery—potted palms—as well as stained or etched glass panels set in the wall on either side of the front door. Victorian-inspired hardware, including electrical faceplates and door hinges, are widely available at local hardware stores. They also can be purchased by mail from The Renovator's Supply in Millers Falls, Massachusetts. If you have a small console table, smother the top with a mass of photographs in Victorian-derived frames—silver, brass, and tortoiseshell or silk, damask, and moire fabrics. Here is the place to highlight an antique piece of silver or a modern bowl emblazoned with Victo-

A ponderous, overscaled hall tree is visually lightened with hats and a straw basket as decorative accessories. To keep the spirit of this small foyer light and airy, the owners have wisely chosen pale paint tones and kept the floor bare.

Robert Perron

Karin Craddock

Too much is never enough when it comes to adding decorative tile. In this hallway, the checkerboard pattern on the floor is juxtaposed with a glazed ceramic medallion pattern. Plainglazed tile is arranged as a frame for hand-painted tiles emblazoned with floral patterns—and the wall tile is treated as if it were wainscoting.

To greet their guests, the owners of this beautiful house descend a stairway covered with an Oriental runner. A built-in window seat is a quiet place to enjoy conversation with departing friends or to drop a coat after a hard day at the office.

Jeffrey Weiss

olive green. Other hat racks authentic to the period are made of light-grained golden oak and brass. Look for originals in antiques stores and at country auctions. An ironstone vase will contrast with the flowers it holds and add Victorian flair, whether it is decorated with a design or is devoid of ornament.

Antique and reproduction Victorian clocks are widely available and make a practical addition to the foyer. The clock may be a simple one or a distinctively shaped "banjo" clock. For an offbeat accessory, shop the flea markets and antiques shops for a walking stick—or an entire collection of them—to place casually in a bamboo or metal umbrella stand or mount on the wall for maximum visual impact.

In lighting, nothing beats a reproduction brass chandelier in an old-fashioned, gaslight design. It adds just the right atmospheric touch to the room. Also appropriate for a country scheme is an antler chandelier, although, because of its large scale, it requires a good-sized room to look its best.

Architectural ornaments supply a true Victorian feeling. Replace molding around modern doors and windows with planks measuring 5 inches wide and contemporary baseboards with wood strips at least 7 inches high. To complete the transformation of a plain entry into a Victorian country foyer, place a large piece of crown molding above the front door. Finishing touches range from brass door hinges to glass and porcelain doorknobs such as those from The Renovators Supply House.

Though presented here in terms of the foyer, many of the ideas for the various design schemes are just as applicable to the foyer's first cousins—the stairway and the hallway. All three serve as "connectors" to get you from one place to another in the house, and all three can be treated in a similiar fashion. For example, the minimalist's mirror in the entry looks just as nice in the hallway. The only difference is that stair landings usually have a window that requires some sort of decorative treatment. In the traditional, eclectic, and even the contemporary scheme, a swag of drapery fabric evocative of Victorian times will suffice. The stair landing, in addition, is an excellent spot to create a small sitting area for quiet conversation or solitary contemplation. In designing a sitting area, however, let modern space-planning rule to insure that the passageway is left unobstructed.

Even a small space like today's foyer can be made visually arresting. It may require some study and advance planning, but every space, the designers assure us, has some rewarding aspect. It could be an interesting architectural detail, an odd angle, or even its small size. "You may have to look hard, but you'll find it," says designer Joseph Pricci of New York City. "Then it merely becomes a matter of how you treat it to emphasize the interesting element."

Peter Paige

CHAPTER TWO

THE KITCHEN

♦　♦　♦　♦　♦

More and more, today's kitchen reflects the vibrancy and warmth of the Victorian spirit. Instead of being merely an antiseptic food-preparation center to get into—and out of—as quickly as possible, the kitchen is assuming a life of its own and becoming a true living space. It is the setting for informal dining in the evening and on weekends. And, with the incorporation of a sitting area near the work space, it is quickly becoming a room for entertaining guests while the cook prepares dinner.

In these respects, the kitchen of the mid-1980s is much like its Victorian counter-part. Though our food preparation area is usually a sleek counter, the Victorians used a large wood table for chopping and other routine tasks. We store our utensils and dinnerware in built-in cabinets; the Victorian kitchen was "furnished," usually with a large dresser and cupboards. The equivalent of today's pantry was the larder, where food was kept cold on slate floors in the decades before electricity. In many modern houses, the kitchen is connected to a service area containing the laundry center. The Victorians had a similar space—the scullery, which was equipped with a sink and pots to launder clothing as well as to trim vegetables. As in many contemporary kitchens, the Victorians often had a comfortable sitting area with carpeting and, sometimes, a large clock.

Windsor chairs at the dining table firmly establish a Victorian tone in this modern, open-plan, kitchen-dining area. The pine floor and oak cabinetry in a tambour finish evocative of wainscoting are less obvious examples that add to the overall look of the room.

Colorful, hand-painted ceramic tiles become the center of attention in the cooking area of an otherwise contemporary kitchen. The whimsical Victorian air created by the tiles is reinforced by beaded paneling on the cabinets above and below.

Karen Bussolini

These similarities make it easy to imbue today's kitchens with a Victorian flavor. Many details can be borrowed from that long-ago era and adapted for modern use:

♦ Practical, easy-to-maintain ceramic tile flooring

♦ Glass-paneled cabinetry

♦ Beaded wainscoting

♦ Marble countertops

♦ Applied ornamentation around light fixtures, baseboards, and chair rails

♦ Chintz upholstery

♦ Brass and porcelain faucets, handles, and other hardware

Modern kitchens take many forms: pass-through, corridor, U-shaped, L-shaped. Yet the arrangement of appliances usually comes in the same configuration: a triangle formed by the refrigerator, cooktop, and sink. This layout enables the cook to literally pivot from one appliance to the other as needs require. This practical approach to space-planning should rule any good kitchen design.

Take advantage of the many modern appliances available today—dishwashers, electric ranges, microwave ovens, and the like—without feeling that they must be camouflaged in a Victorian manner. Contemporary appliances frequently have a sculptural quality that enhances their innate practicality. There is no need to conceal a refrigerator behind old armoire doors. That just adds an extra—and unnecessary—obstacle to its practicality. "I adore decorating, but you get too precious and silly when you try to hide the appliances," says designer Catherine Stephens of Long Island, New York.

Instead, blend modern appliances and Victorian details with color—white appliances in a white kitchen, almond-colored ones, for example, in a beige color scheme. This unifies old and new without hindering function. Choosing appropriate paint colors has been greatly simplified in recent years, following extensive research into the Victorian palette. Several paint companies now offer colors in Victorian-inspired hues. And two companies sell paint colors that include authentic reproductions. Fuller-O'Brien has introduced a collection of 70 hues called "The Palette of Cape May Victorian Colors," in honor of the seacoast resort in New Jersey renowned for its concentration of 600 vintage Victorian houses, many of which have been restored to their original grandeur. Sherwin-Williams has long offered a selection of forty

Karen Bussolini

From the cooking area, opposite page, the beaded paneling is repeated as wainscoting that extends around the room. It softens the contemporary elements—a center cooking island, track lighting, plastic laminate countertops, and modern appliances.

authentic colors that has been utilized in historic restorations. The range of colors in both of these collections is sufficient for almost any taste—ranging from rich, dark browns to midnight blues and emerald greens to very pale tones with just a blush of tint.

To maintain contemporary functioning with a Victorian flair, concentrate on furniture and backgrounds—floor, ceiling, and walls—as well as cabinetry, accessories, and architectural ornamentation.

TRADITIONAL

Just-baked bread, Devon cream, fresh eggs—these are the images and smells of both the traditional and the romantic kitchen. The secret in this environment is to choose furniture that reflects fine craftsmanship, attention to detail, and the solidity of the Victorian era. Nothing establishes a Victorian mood in these settings like finely grained oak furniture and cabinetry. A large, round table with ball-and-claw feet surrounded by Windsor chairs were staples in the middle-class, nineteenth-century kitchen and can easily be included in a modern kitchen.

Golden oak is just one choice. Wicker chairs in a natural finish, bentwood, and Eastlake pieces can imbue the kitchen with warmth while creating a light, airy feeling. Victorian cottage furniture, circa 1880, includes dressers that would be most appropriate in a kitchen today. A natural wood stain embellished with painted floral motifs accommodates modern tastes.

Glass-fronted, wall-hung cabinets in oak reinforce the Victorian atmosphere and inform you at a glance of their contents. Cabinet doors with glass panels, however, must be cleaned more frequently than those made of solid wood. So, if low-maintenance is a priority, you are probably better off choosing the latter. As another option you can take the doors off and leave the shelving open.

Because work surfaces should be easy to clean, ceramic tile, butcher block, and marble make excellent countertops. Ceramic tile also is the most practical floor covering. Small, hexagon-shaped tiles immediately impart an old-fashioned feeling while four-inch squares offer a more contemporary alternative. To break up the expanse of ceramic and create a pattern that adds visual texture and interest, insert a strip of wood every four tiles or so. Or, cover the floor entirely with a natural-stained wood that matches a butcher block countertop. A polyurethaned oak floor is easy to care for and adds warmth to a kitchen.

Wallpaper in a Victorian-styled kitchen might include a pattern from the "Fields of Flowers" collection by Thomas Strahan Company, which is composed of small-scale flowers on a neutral

background. Many designers do not recommend applying wallpaper between the overhead cabinetry and the work counters, however, as it tends to visually break up the wall. Instead, the same type of ceramic tile placed on the floor can be used on the wall to add a sense of continuity and help unify the overall design scheme. A rich creamy white paint is also appropriate, particularly when woodwork is painted a contrasting light color. The white expands the sense of spaciousness and lightness in the room and gives it a fresh clean look that is important in the food preparation areas.

Norman McGrath

Neil Lorimer/EWA

An expanse of stained wood recalls the nineteenth century in this traditionally designed kitchen. The pressed-tin ceiling, paddle fan, wall sconces, and simple drapery add to the Victorian atmosphere.

An array of classically inspired china is right at home on a tall breakfront topped with crown molding. Besides keeping the impressive pieces close at hand, the breakfront doubles as an elegant display case.

If the kitchen is sufficiently screened from the sightline of neighbors, highlight graceful old double-hung windows by leaving them bare. When window treatments are needed, shutters add a custom-made look. You can make them yourself; Design Portfolio of Takoma Park, Maryland, sells plans with which you can build insulated shutters that can be covered with a Victorian-inspired fabric.

Sweet calico curtains with matching tiebacks evoke another kind of Victorian feeling. The Suzy Curtain Company takes a slightly more elaborate approach by manufacturing solid color

In a renovated kitchen in Connecticut, etched-glass cabinet inserts by artist Sandy Moore and a lacy window treatment visually soften the monochromatic color scheme and severe architectural lines of the center cooking island.

Robert Perron

An unusual stained-glass panel in the door imbues this traditional kitchen with an air of drama. It is framed by flouncy window treatments evocative of delicate lace.

In this restored kitchen, the sloped ceiling soars upward creating space for a paddle fan, reminiscent of the Victorian Age. In winter, the fan helps draw warm air down from the top of the room for even heating.

curtains trimmed with macramé in the firm's new "Brussells" collection. For a lighter Victorian touch, invest in curtains made entirely of lace. These can be either period pieces that you may discover at an antique shop or one of the many new machine-made lines. Larger department stores such as B. Altman in New York City stock curtains resembling Victorian drawnwork. In this technique, threads are pulled out of the fabric to create a "negative" stripe, curtain treatment that lends the kitchen an air of delicacy. Yet the curtains are made of contemporary easy-care fabrics that can be laundered with little effort.

Accessories are important and can be fun in the kitchen, but they should be functional. Among the pretty and practical items possible are enamelware pitchers, cups, and platters as well as rolling pins, copper pots, and muffin tins with interesting Victorian designs. Cumberland General Store, a mail-order house in Crossville, Tennessee, stocks a number of tins in various motifs—hearts, fruits, and playing cards.

Although they might not seem practical, kerosene lamps in metal or glass help strike an old-fashioned note when dining informally. After the food is prepared, turn off the contemporary fluorescent fixtures and enjoy a meal softly illuminated by five or six lamps placed on the table. The lamps often can be found at flea markets for as little as five dollars. And now, their biggest aesthetic drawback has been eliminated with the development of odorless kerosene.

CONTEMPORARY AND ECLECTIC

Because of their similarities in materials and colors, contemporary and eclectic kitchen design schemes can be "Victorianized" the same way. Wallpaper, such as one in a William Morris design from Clarence House, Brunschwig & Fils, or Cowtan & Tout or a light-colored floral or trellis pattern, is widely available at retail stores across the country. "Wildgrasses," a pattern designed by Cindi Mufson for Tiffany Prints is available through Collins & Aikman and has a rich terra-cotta ground with thin cream stripes.

Although the Victorian flavor can also be added with fabric, designers generally recommend against using it in the kitchen because it requires frequent cleaning. Tile is an excellent alternative because of its innate Victorian feeling and its easy-care characteristics.

In windows and cabinetry an abundant use of glass accentuates both the contemporary and eclectic feeling of today and that of the Victorian Age. The glass can take a number of forms. If you want to leave the windows bare but are concerned about privacy, consider frosted or etched glass. Other options include beveled, leaded, or stained glass, which can also be incorporated into cabinet doors, lending these important elements an air of Victorian authenticity.

The wood frames of the cabinets, windows, and doors can be painted a rich creamy white or a pale beige to highlight the glass. Then top the cabinets with six-inch thick crown molding painted the same color. If the kitchen is large, you can safely add other wall elements similar to those discussed in "The Foyer"—wide baseboard molding, a chair rail, wainscoting, and paneling painted a light color.

Of course, there are other ways to add a Victorian flavor in a contemporary or eclectic kitchen. Rough-sawn oak flooring often makes the floor the focal point; ceramic tile flooring, especially when paired with a pine hutch, creates a sense of contradiction that increases visual interest. This freestanding piece in a natural finish can be set near other wood cabinetry painted a light color. Visit a local salvage yard to see if you can find cabinetry for sale that can be recycled. Perhaps there are several partial cabinets that can be pieced together to form a whole one. This "new"

A nineteenth-century light fixture illuminates a table and chairs from the 1920s in this traditional kitchen, above. A lace tablecloth and late Victorian hutch add a nineteenth-century flavor to a renovated kitchen, which incorporates a contemporary sloped ceiling, right.

Randy O'Rourke

Karen Bussolini

A sturdy oak table, bentwood chairs, and an expansive hutch bring a Victorian sensibility to a thoroughly eclectic setting blending vinyl flooring and wainscoting.

The juxtaposition of a marble table and tile floor creates a design tension enlivened by contemporary open shelving, casual chairs, and a commercially inspired refrigerator.

Phillip Ennis

Richard M. Ross

Square ceramic floor tile brings a contemporary feeling to this renovated kitchen. The traditionally styled cabinetry adds an appealing accent to the room.

Though often considered too visually severe for a kitchen, the gray palette of a minimalist designer forms a perfect backdrop for a wood workspace and dainty lace curtains in this product-advertising photograph from Rue de France.

Courtesy of Rue de France

cabinet can then be painted to conceal the alterations. With this approach you get the charm of authenticity that many designers insist new cabinetry can't match.

Wicker and rattan accessories blend into contemporary kitchens, for example, when straw baskets are used to display fruit and vegetables. An indoor herb garden can be grown right on the windowsill in baskets or terra-cotta-colored clay pots. Shiny copper cooking utensils and wooden cooking spoons become accessories that add to the Victorian flavor, as does an old set of kitchen canisters to store flour, sugar, and salt. Delightful designs in metal and ceramic are sold in junk shops, while new reproductions are available at kitchen specialty outlets and many department stores. If you collect old Victorian water pitchers, platters, mugs, and cups, display them atop the overhead cabinetry. Old ceramic crocks make excellent flower vases and can store utensils.

MINIMAL

The walls are an excellent starting point in giving a kitchen designed in the minimalist vein a Victorian feeling. Tongue-and-groove slatting resembling lathe work can be applied to the walls. Painted a rich white, this technique adds texture without requiring wallpaper. The slatting can also be placed on the ceiling. When mounted on the cabinet doors as well, the slatting will make them seem to disappear, as if the woodwork were built-in.

Old-time charm and efficient, contemporary functioning blend seamlessly in a kitchen renovated by architect Blue Minges. The secret—a deft mixing of a woodburning stove, warehouse lighting fixtures, modern ceramic tile, and a Parsons-style table with a genuine butcher-block work surface.

Robert Perron

The wall treatment can be much simpler. A wallpaper border looks smart around the top of the wall. The border pattern can take any number of forms: a reproduction William Morris design, a paisley pattern, or solid colors in grayish green, persimmon, or paler red. Solid hues can be incorporated into a stencil design to create architectural interest and a sense of detailing where none exists.

Though the ardent minimalist prefers gray industrial carpeting, it isn't very practical in the kitchen. An oak floor, however, will look quite striking and is practical when protected by several coats of polyurethane. In contrast to the traditional approach, it can be painted a rich brown or bleached for a lighter appearance. Another finish for a wood floor is decorative—paint it to resemble marble with light gray veins. Or try a checkerboard design on a tile floor, enlivened with a small diamond motif painted where the four corners of the tile meet. A linoleum floor in alternating black-and-white or green-and-white squares adds sparkle to the minimalist scheme.

The addition of an unexpected material or color enlivens a minimal room by injecting a slight sense of contradiction. For example, designer Tim Romanello suggests constructing a banquette in a dining area that is upholstered in a solid rose-colored cotton. This look can then be softened with small pillows covered in a chintz fabric with green or cinnamon backgrounds and a light floral pattern.

Varying the furniture is another way to add visual contrast. In an informal dining area, bamboo or faux-bamboo, now found in many antiques shops and in reproduction, go well in a minimalist scheme. Natural-finish wicker is authentically Victorian and, in a spare minimalist design, lends a sculptural feeling. Then, there are pieces that were never intended for the kitchen but work quite well there. Try wire garden furniture that is softened—figuratively and literally—with glazed chintz cushions. Though not strictly Victorian, Adirondack furniture corresponds to the era

Courtesy of Motif

Fitted against a backdrop of nineteenth-century inspired paneling and a Victorian Gothic window treatment, the thoroughly modern refrigerator and hardware set an eclectic tone.

The timeless appeal of traditional design is enhanced by elements drawn from the Victorian Age—a beautiful round table, airy lace curtains, and a practical ceramic tile floor.

Jeffrey Weiss

and can be incorporated into a minimalist scheme. Again, soften their visual impact with cushions in a light ground of celadon green and flower patterns in tones of rose, blue, lavender, and yellow from Lee Jofa Inc. Another upholstery option is a Rose Cumming fabric with a pattern of urns, garlands, and flowers.

Accessories should, indeed, be kept minimal. But if you collect Victorian-era plates, platters, and jars, display them judiciously. They will add a sense of humanity and warmth often missing in this design scheme. Other collectibles work well, too, including small antique bottles holding flowers and Victorian-styled copper cooking utensils.

COUNTRY

Nothing establishes a Victorian mood in a country-style kitchen quicker or better than architectural ornamentation. Fine cabinetry embellished with crown molding and ceiling beams set the mood instantly. For a truly authentic touch, acquire old oak cabinets from a salvage yard or recycle some old oak planks and assemble custom cabinets of your own. The crown molding will help fit them into today's kitchen and further the Victorian motif. Another approach is to have a craft-oriented designer such as Beverly Ellsley of Westport, Connecticut, plan new custom cabinets. Usually these are made of pine, a wood that Ms. Ellsley says takes a stain and paint better than the new oak available. The configuration of Victorian-inspired cabinets is different, too. Wider rails on the doors add a greater sense of mass and are historically more correct than contemporary stock cabinets. The panels bordered by the rails can be made of wood, mirror, or glass, either etched or beveled.

To reinforce the Victorian feeling, select countertops and work surfaces made of tile and marble, as fitting in a country kitchen as in a more traditional one. For modern convenience with an old-fashioned look in a country kitchen, you may want to choose the DuPont Corian work surface that is colored throughout so scratches won't show. A truly nostalgic touch is the honed marble that was used on old drugstore counters. It is gray, with veins in either a darker gray or white. The term "honed" means the marble is not polished but bears a matte finish for a timeworn look.

For maximum impact, Victorian furniture in a country kitchen should be oak or pine. Bentwood or oak Windsor chairs extend the Victorian theme. Compatible modern pieces—a Cesca chair, for example—can be substituted to create an interesting look. If there is sufficient space, place an old scrubbed pine table in the work area and use it as a contemporary work island. This adds a Victorian touch; at the same time, it creates space to chop and mince, and store a variety of cooking utensils.

Integrated with new and old photographs, a nineteenth-century circular tray doubles as both a serving piece and as a decorative accessory when hung on a paneled wall in a country-style kitchen.

Scrubbed pine is the essence of today's country look. Here, a hanging kitchen cupboard is decorated with bounty of the Victorian Age—a collection of tin canisters, a teapot, and an assortment of plates, cups, and saucers. Dried herbs form a beautiful frame for the cupboard and are close at hand when needed to season meals.

Jeffrey Weiss

Reminiscent of a colonial keeping-room, this elegant version of a country kitchen bears the subtle influence of the Victorian Age. The bentwood café chairs arranged around the table provide an undeniable touch of class.

Victorian ceramics—pitchers, serving bowls, figurines, and other table accessories—find a cozy home in the corner pine hutch of a relaxed country kitchen.

Robert Perron

Keith Scott Morton

An old country-style gas stove is the dominant element in a rustic kitchen. It is supplemented by architectural detailing, including nineteenth-century New England paneling and a wood-framed window. The owner has carried through the Victorian theme in the decorating by adding an etched-glass hanging lamp, an old lantern, a coffee grinder, a metal coffee pot on the cooktop, and an old bread box.

A collection of odds and ends, including a Victorian child's chair, a twig wreath, and a framed photograph, become a still-life study in the corner of a comfortable kitchen.

The addition of ceiling beams also imbues a country-style kitchen with a Victorian flair. They can be painted, boxed with plasterboard, or left bare. The use of ceiling beams can be taken a step further by installing cross beams that create the effect of a deeply coffered ceiling. Then, the entire ceiling can be painted a solid light color. Or, the beams and the ceiling can be painted in contrasting tones, further highlighting the architectural ornamentation and making it the focal point of the entire kitchen.

Ceramic tile, brick, wood, slate, and bluestone are excellent flooring materials for a country kitchen designed in the Victorian manner. In the eating area, these can be covered with an Oriental rug or one of its rural cousins; some of the more charming country alternatives include rag and hooked rugs bearing patterns of dogs, cats, farm scenes, and flowers. Most of the hooked rugs are less than four-by-six feet and many of them are frequently shaped like a half-moon, which, very subtly, adds to their visual appeal.

Wall treatments include the classic nineteenth-century approach: beaded wainscoting painted the same light color as the walls. If you cover the floor with ceramic tile, bring it up the wall to waist level. For a dramatic touch around appliances and cooking center, extend the tile all the way to the ceiling. The walls can then be painted and embellished with molding in a contrasting color.

The best accessories have a slightly primitive feel. This is a great opportunity to indulge in spatterware, as well as glazed ceramic spongeware in blue-and-white or green-and-white. These are readily available in department stores, kitchen supply centers, and by mail from outfits such as Cumberland General-store. Silver is fitting, too, as long as it is simple in design. Save your more ornate pieces for the dining room.

A WORD ABOUT ACCESSORIES

Inventories of kitchens from the Victorian era reveal a wide variety of serving pieces and miscellaneous items such as doorstops, baking molds, and copper cooking pans. A number of these Victorian items fit equally well into today's design schemes, depending on your personal preferences.

The early middle-class Victorian kitchen usually included a clock. Frequently, it was a long-case clock, or what is often called a grandfather clock, based on an eighteenth- or nineteenth-century design. Later in the Victorian Age, the long-case clock was replaced in many kitchens with a pub clock, which has a round face in a short case that hangs on the wall. Simple, even plain in their design, these clocks can be found today in junk shops and at country yard and antiques sales.

Tea trays are both decorative and functional. Earlier pieces were more primitive and most commonly made of wood. Later in the nineteenth century, the trays were constructed of papier-mâché—sometimes in elaborate designs—and inlaid with mother-of-pearl. Look for these in more exclusive antiques shops. They also are carried by wholesalers that cater directly to designers and architects. Better antiques shops and wholesalers are also excellent sources for doorstops and boot scrapers. Many are in imaginative designs such as lions and other exotic animals, in cast iron painted black.

Kitchen molds for butter and jelly came in a wide variety of designs and materials—wood, earthenware, tin, pewter, and copper—emblazoned with shell, leaf, rose, and fern designs. These are available as reproductions if you can't find originals.

Cooking pots of the nineteenth century are as functional today as they were a hundred years ago. The most beautiful Victorian cooking pans were made of copper with carved wooden handles. If you don't want copper, other metalware in the Victorian kitchen might include brass candlesticks and candlesnuffers.

Ceramic cooking and serving pieces reached new heights of beauty in the Victorian Age, and, fortunately, survive today in antiques shops. Mocha earthenware was fabricated into tankards, bowls, jugs, and other dishes. It is distinguished by a brown or white ground decorated with dark brown or blue marbling or patterns in naturalistic forms, primarily seaweed and feathers.

Victorian kitchen accessories are so beautiful that they belong front and center. In this setting, they are smartly arranged on a hanging wall cabinet and a large-scale hutch. An overhead track keeps pots and pans close at hand yet out of the way of the cook. Stenciling around windows and doorways adds to the Victorian spirit of the room and contrasts nicely with modern appliances and Mexican tile.

Randy O'Rourke

A staggering assortment of Victorian platters, bowls, and teapots finds a comfortable niche on contemporary open shelving in the corner of this beautiful and functional kitchen. The accessories are so eye-catching that they obscure the difference in materials—butcher block and plastic laminate countertops—as well as the contrast between the open shelves and traditional overhead cabinetry.

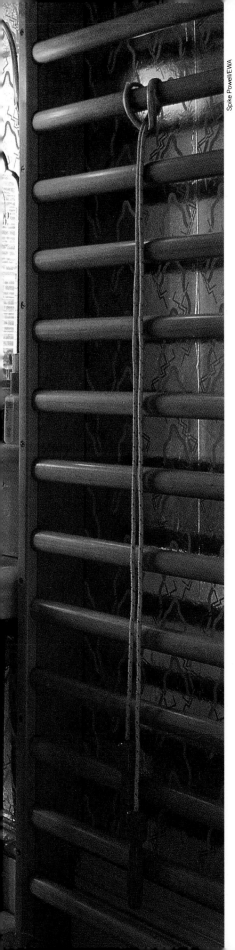

CHAPTER THREE

THE BATHROOM

◆ ◆ ◆ ◆ ◆

The modern-style bathroom is one of the Victorians' most notable inventions. For much of the age, sanitary facilities consisted of a chamber pot and a pitcher and bowl on a washstand in a corner of the bedroom. As indoor plumbing was developed, a small room—the water closet—was set aside for the toilet. Gradually, the bathroom grew in size and in the number of amenities it incorporated. By the late 1880s bathing and grooming facilities occupied an entire room and included most of the fixtures that we are now using today.

Plumbing catalogs from the late nineteenth century illustrate bathrooms that are quaintly dated, but that are familiar in appearance. Tubs were both freestanding and framed in wood. Shower enclosures, though not very popular with the Victorians, consisted of a circular curtain in the center of the tub with the shower head above. Some manufacturers incorporated a three-sided shower stall at one end of the tub. The basin was set into a wood cabinet with a one-foot-tall splashback. Above that, an oval mirror for grooming was flanked by two gaslights, and between the vanity and the tub was a seat-and-foot bath. The toilet often was an elaborate porcelain fixture emblazoned with decorative patterns of dolphins and other sea creatures. The water tank had a long pull cord, and was suspended from the wall near the ceiling.

Nineteenth-century plumbing fixtures—a deep tub and an elevated sink—are the heart of this bathroom. Note other Victorian features, such as the crown molding, high baseboard, and lovely interior window shutters.

The middle-class Victorian bathroom often had all the trimmings. A kilim-style carpet covered a ceramic tile floor, and wainscoting was deeply carved with rectangular motifs. Floral design wallpaper borders were applied around the tops of the walls, and the ceiling was often decorated with latticework.

The bathroom window was frequently quite large, and filled with a colored leaded glass that admitted softly filtered light into the room, but retained privacy. A gas chandelier with two globes illuminated the entire bathroom.

Color schemes were an interesting blend of light and dark tones. Woodwork was invariably dark. It was offset, however, by buff-colored walls above the wainscoting, while tile floors and porcelain fixtures were white.

Many of these elements still practical today include:

♦ Pedestal sinks and oversized tubs with claw feet

♦ Wood surrounds for contemporary basins and tubs

♦ Reproduction Victorian hardware

♦ Small ballroom chair

♦ Bamboo or faux-bamboo towel stand

♦ Botanical prints

♦ An antique mirror or contemporary mirror in an old frame

♦ Cool ceramic tile flooring

The most effective way to establish a Victorian feeling in any style bathroom is with old-fashioned fixtures and hardware. New fixtures designed in the Victorian manner abound at retail from manufacturers such as Kohler, American Standard, and Barclay Products, Ltd. Tubs are large with claw feet, while sinks are set on pedestals. New pedestal sinks imbued with the flavor of the old are also manufactured by Sherle Wagner and The Sink Factory in Berkeley, California.

Original fixtures are sold at architectural salvage yards, including Urban Archaeology in New York and The Wrecking Bar in Atlanta and Dallas. But many designers insist that the absolutely cheapest way to get an authentic fixture is to visit the town dump in suburbs of older cities where old fixtures are often discarded.

These items get jettisoned primarily for two reasons: a fitting, perhaps a handle, has broken, and the homeowners, not realizing that it can be repaired quickly and inexpensively, have thrown the entire tub or sink out; or perfectly functional old fixtures are removed during remodeling by homeowners and contractors who neither recognize nor appreciate their aesthetic or financial value. Unless damaged during removal, fixtures are usually in operating condition and will only need new fittings. Extensive lines of new fittings made to the specifications of the old tubs and sinks are

In a cramped bathroom, the basin has been placed in the only available space to make a corner vanity. The exposed plumbing dates the fixture from the nineteenth century, yet hints of today's industrial style in contemporary interior design.

The classical columns of Rome and Greece have been adapted to the Age of Indoor Plumbing. This striking pedestal sink is fitted with porcelain and set beneath an ornate mirror.

Richard M. Ross

In this bathroom, an unsightly vanity has been skirted with crisp fabric. The claw-footed tub remains with all of its enduring charm. Untouched, too, is the architectural detailing, which has been painted a contrasting color. The simple and straightforward treatment of this old bathroom is inexpensive and within the budget of even the most cost-conscious home remodeler. And ideas such as the claw-footed tub, vanity skirt, and eye-commanding painted detailing can be adapted into many modern houses with ease.

Jeffrey Weiss

Sculptural and practical, an old bentwood washstand dominates a corner of a traditionally styled bathroom. Besides containing a basin and mirror, the stand includes space to hang towels conveniently close to the adjacent shower area. Striped floral wallpaper and louvered doors that open into the wet portion of the bathroom reinforce the oldtime flavor, as does the wicker basket.

available from various companies such as The Renovators Supply.

A simple basin instead of a pedestal sink will provide you with more storage room in the bathroom. New basins based on Victorian designs are produced by The Sink Factory and Reid S. Watson. These can be installed in several ways. Reminiscent of the Victorian era, basins can be encased with a wood surround made of beaded or paneled wainscoting. Or, they can be set into an old cupboard, dresser, or dining room sideboard that will supply extra storage space keeping towels, cosmetics, hair dryers and other contemporary grooming aids concealed from sight. However, be aware that the storage capacity will be reduced because the furniture must also accommodate plumbing.

Because the bathroom is inherently a wet, humid environment, wood finishes need some kind of protection. In a windowless room, an exhaust fan will prevent wood from being damaged by exposure to steam. It's probably best to seal wood finishes with polyurethane. Apply two or three coats for an area exposed to frequent water spills such as a wood basin surround. "If you sand each layer before you apply the next, you'll have a nice smooth finish like that on bar tops," advises Robert Denning of Denning & Fourcade, a leading New York City interior design firm.

If you use a new vanity, a painted finish will make it look old. A wood-grain design is appropriate for a traditional bath, while a pattern of flowers and leaves goes well with an eclectic or romantic motif. A faux-marble finish will complement a minimal or contemporary scheme. Of course, the finish you choose will depend upon your own design scheme.

Dress up a mundane modern vanity inexpensively by skirting it with a Victorian-inspired fabric. Tightly shirred or pleated around the edge of the fixture, the fabric conceals the vanity but does not hinder access to the storage area and plumbing below. Excellent fabric choices are patterned chintz or eyelet. If you'd like, everything can be coordinated with matching shower curtains and window coverings, creating a tailored look that reflects a mastery of detail.

In almost any design scheme, wallpaper can create a feeling of nostalgia. If you have a freestanding tub, wallpaper also can be applied around that fixture. Many wallpapers available today have special water-resistant finishes that increase their practicality. Because of concern about damage from dampness, many people refuse to use wallpaper at all in the bathroom. They are afraid that over time, it will peel off the surface. Such concerns are not warranted if the paper is applied correctly, says interior designer Bennett Weinstock of Philadelphia. "You don't have to be apprehensive if the paper is sized correctly and installed properly by a competent paper-hanger," he says. As an alternative, many wallpaper patterns are sold in vinyl form.

Wainscoting, another classic Victorian wall treatment, is also appropriate for today. In fact, wainscoting is often included in many new houses—from less expensive contractor models to custom residences. It's available in two basic configurations—tongue-and-groove and as paneling. Both varieties are sold in lumberyards.

The simplest way to treat wainscoting decoratively is to paint it the same color as the rest of the room. Or, in true Victorian spirit, you can paint it in a complementary color—one directly opposite on the color wheel. Painting the wood also shields it from moisture. In recent years, however, many designers have been leaving the wainscoting natural, applying a coat of varnish or polyurethane to keep the wood safe from water damage.

Wainscoting can be applied around all walls, except in the shower area. In standard five-by-seven-foot bathrooms, designers recommend bringing the wainscoting only thirty-six inches up the wall to prevent it from visually overwhelming the room. It can be applied more generously in larger bathrooms, sometimes extending five feet up the wall. To create a custom detailed look, cut into the wainscoting leaving space for the bathroom mirror.

Homeowners who prefer easy-care bathrooms often eschew wood wainscoting for plastic laminate. This material is produced by Formica Corporation and Wilsonart, to name two of the largest manufacturers, in a wide variety of colors—from dark tones such as hunter green to antiseptic white. In between these two extremes are a number of pastels that will complement any color

The placement of a shell dish with scented soaps next to lace and old perfume bottles unmistakably sets a romantic tone in a corner of an old bathroom, left. Though the bathroom above looks old, it is actually a new interpretation of the Victorian style. A modern pedestal sink is backed with beaded wainscoting beneath a mirror in a simple frame and a swath of floral wallpaper.

An old buffet has been converted into a vanity for use in this eclectic bathroom. Shelves that once held glassware now store extra towels, and the top has been altered to accommodate the basin. The vanity is at the heart of an artfully composed setting that manages to incorporate contrasting floor tile, patterned wallpaper, a formal drapery treatment, and a Queen Anne chair. Wall sconces on both sides of the mirror illuminate the owner's face for safety when shaving.

scheme. Plastic laminate in a tambour design is the closest to tongue-and-groove wainscoting and is often specified by many designers for restaurants decorated around a Victorian theme.

Stenciling can blend into any design motif, too. The effect may be subtle with only a border stenciled on the walls just below the ceiling as a frieze. Complex stencil patterns should be applied by a professional. These trained craftsmen are not as difficult to locate as you might think. Many painters and sculptors supplement their income by painting decorative finishes. Designers frequently enlist their services on projects. Or you can consult your local

fine arts museum for the names of artists who do stencil work in your area. Local schools offering art courses are another souce for quality work by either faculty members or students. If these are not practical alternatives, contact the nearest art-supply store and ask for names of artists. Stenciling also is an excellent do-it-yourself project. Many craft and hobby stores sell stencil kits that include the paints, patterns, and instructions you need to get started.

The application of a wallpaper border at the top of the walls can create the same effect as stenciling. But unless you are skilled at

Phillip Ennis

The owner of this house has fitted the bathroom with shelving that keeps reading materials close at hand. A studylike ambience is heightened by an old floor lamp and end table. Wall paneling contrasts with sleek industrial-style carpeting in this multifunctional room.

The Design Council

Delicate arrays of flowers on this tile reflect the Victorians' commitment to exquisite craftsmanship.

paper-hanging, this is best done by a professional. Both Scalamandre Silks and Schumacher manufacture collections of Victorian wallpaper borders you can buy. They're based on original designs copied from actual samples of Victorian wallpapers called documents.

In the bathrooms of many older houses and apartments, unsightly, often broken, white tiles extend halfway up the wall. An effective yet inexpensive treatment to camouflage them is to apply epoxy in a pattern that simulates wood-graining. Besides hiding the dated tiles, this approach creates an instant impression of wainscoting that reinforces the Victorian feeling.

Ceramic tile flooring is common to almost all bathroom design schemes and is one of the most versatile floor treatments. It can be patterned and color-coordinated. Two other alternative floor treatments are patterned tiles and wood. Imported from Belgium and France, patterned tiles often are hand-painted with flowers and other naturalistic motifs making them appropriate for Victorian-inspired bathrooms. One of the best known sources for patterned tiles is Country Floors in New York City. Oak and pine floors have become popular for bathrooms in recent years due, in part, to the new finishes such as polyurethane that increase their practicality.

Victorian hardware in a range of metal finishes and porcelain can be ordered from manufacturers such as Artistic Brass, Chicago Faucets, and Cirecast of San Francisco. Brian F. Leo, a craftsman who lives in Richfield, Minnesota, will reproduce custom hardware based on your design. Reproduction hardware is sold by speciality stores including Kraft Hardware in New York City, Crawford's Old House Store in Waukesha, Wisconsin, and Litchfield House in Roxbury, Connecticut.

In planning the lighting for the bathroom, professional designers urge their clients to choose contemporary sources. Good bathroom design generally requires an overhead backlight as well as fixtures on either side of the mirror. That way, the face is illuminated from three angles. There is, however, a place for decorative Victorian lighting. Fitted with rheostats, or dimmers, the fixtures can effectively create the Victorian atmosphere you want.

Larger bathrooms today sometimes double as receiving and entertaining rooms. One New York couple has created a Victorian nook complete with the bathroom facilities and a sitting area—all encased in glass—along one wall of their apartment. They have been quoted as saying that they still wince when they invite friends over for "cocktails in the bathroom."

The typical bathroom, of course, isn't so elaborate nor is there a genuine need for such plush facilities. But furniture—whether it is a console or a wicker bench to store extra towels—can enhance

Middle-class Victorian houses had all the amenities. Witness this bathroom that even includes a fireplace set between the toilet tank and the wall-hung basin, right. Wall sconces add an air of elegance to this utilitarian room as does the high baseboard molding. A hanging cupboard finds new purpose as a bathroom vanity, below. Its dark stain contrasts nicely with the lightly patterned floral wallpaper.

both the atmosphere and the functioning of the space. Appropriate furniture for a bathroom varies according to its use, size, and design scheme.

For some specific suggestions on furnishings as well as lighting, surface treatments, and accessories, each design style is discussed individually below.

TRADITIONAL

Victorian fixtures look especially at home in a bathroom designed in the traditional vein. Claw-footed tubs and pedestal sinks fit naturally into this design scheme, as do patterned pedestal sinks by Sherle Wagner. Even new fixtures can be imbued with the spirit of the old when they are encased in wood and surrounded with molding to create a detailed finished look.

If you have a new sink and vanity, soften its visual impact with skirting. There are at least two methods. You can tightly gather patterned glazed chintz or use simple panels of eyelet embroidery that hang to the floor. Contrasting welting keeps the skirt in place and adds to the tailored look.

Many designers convert furniture originally intended for other rooms into a vanity to hold a new basin. Robert Denning often uses old bedroom bureaus and dining room sideboards, while Philadelphia designer Bennett Weinstock has employed kitchen cupboards. Weinstock also suggests painting a new vanity in a wood grain so that it will look like a regency chest or having a vanity custom-built in wood, then applying a decorative finish.

If you have sufficient storage, substitute a mirror for the medicine chest. The mirror can be an antique with a beautifully carved frame or a new mirror in an old frame picked up at a flea market. Designer Leah Lenney of Larchmont, New York, believes in recycling. She has had mirrors removed from the medicine cabinet door and cut to fit old frames.

In a traditional scheme, shower enclosures often present an aesthetic problem. You can leave glass shower doors as they are without trying to camouflage them, or you can have the glass etched by an artist like Sandy Moore of Guilford, Connecticut. Shower curtains, however, look more familiar in a traditional bath. To make them the focal point of the room, add a valance that extends below the rod with chintz tightly shirred as if it were a window drapery. On the shower rod place a matching or contrasting chintz fabric that reaches to the floor as the decorative curtain. Behind that add a plastic liner. Use matching or contrasting tiebacks, as well as tassels and other dressmaker details to accent the shower curtain.

Hardware selection for fixtures has been greatly expanded as

Bruce Glass

Traditionalism has been updated in a Houston, Texas, house. The old-style toilet tank looks right at home with striped wallpaper, a pedestal basin in a shell design, and wall sconces with glass globes.

In a contemporary New York City loft, the artist-owner harked back to the nineteenth century in planning her bathroom. Among her exciting finds: beaded wall paneling, old mirrors, light fixtures, and a towel rack hung from a section of chair railing. An old pitcher-and-bowl set complements the Manhattan skyline.

Peter Loppcher

designers rediscover the nineteenth century. Many that are infused with a Victorian feeling are sold at local hardware stores in brass, bronze, and nickel-plate. Chicago Faucets offers an entire line of Victorian-style gooseneck faucets and handles. Formerly used by hospitals as doctors' wash-up sinks, these fixtures have become so popular with designers that the company now offers them as a separate category within their product line.

Wainscoting fits naturally into the traditional bathroom, whether it is the tongue-and-groove or panel variety. In this setting it looks superb when topped with crown molding painted a matching or slightly darker color beneath chintz fabric or floral pattern wallpaper. In place of wainscoting, add a chair rail. Paint the area of the wall below the rail and wallpaper the area above, or install different wallpapers above and below that are coordinated either in color or in design motif. A larger-scale pattern is usually better for the lower half, but can be used above the chair rail if the pattern on the lower half stands out in its coloration. Beautiful French-inspired wallpapers that lend a Victorian air with their small patterning are available at retail from Pierre Deux in New York City. Roger Arlington, formerly Papier Paints, a wholesale trade source for architects and designers, sells a paper called

"Jane" that has a grid design formed by leaves with luscious little flowers in the center. Though available in several colorways, the pink-and-green combination is a favorite among traditionally inclined designers.

Fabrics are an excellent alternative to wallpaper on a bathroom wall and an option that greatly softens the room visually. Splashy floral patterns in chintz on a light ground go especially well in a traditional bathroom. An unusual chintz but one true to the Victorian spirit is the "Haymarket" pattern from The Twigs in California. Inspired by the old open-air market of the same name in Boston, this farm vegetable pattern includes a number of colors. For a touch of true luxury, use a glossy silk in a brilliant red or green and paint all the woodwork white.

Ceramic tile can create a solid color floor, or it can be enlivened with borders and a pattern. White is the standard choice, but ceramic tile also comes in an array of colors appropriate for a traditional bathroom, including strong red, green, pink, olive, and brown. You can devise a pattern by alternating those colors with tiles that are white or cream color. Borders can be created by placing tiles along the wall in solid or alternating colors. If you use a patterned tile, border the floor with undecorated tiles in the

Richard Chestnut

An old tub takes on an air of sculptural elegance when framed by three walls papered with an eye-catching pattern. Old tubs similar to this one are sold by architectural recycling companies located throughout the country. They are also available for free at many municipal disposal sites in older urban areas.

same ground color. In a small bathroom, designers suggest limiting the border to a single row of tiles. Double rows are nice in a larger bathroom for the framing effect they give the floor.

Wood floors can be left natural, stained to complement the color scheme, or embellished with a pattern. If the floor consists of random planks, stain alternating boards in contrasting colors checkerboard-style. For a truly elegant floor treatment, lacquer the wood to match your overall color scheme.

Ceiling decoration works well in the traditional bathroom. A wallpapered ceiling pleasantly surprises friends when they enter the room, yet because it is above the normal sightline it remains unobtrusive. A ceiling can be papered in either matching or contrasting patterns with the walls, or it can be applied above bare walls. A geometric pattern forming a grid will give the room the feeling of having a coffered ceiling. A wallpaper border on the ceiling goes well here, too, as it "defines" the surface, thus visually unifying the entire room.

If the bathroom is small, you may prefer to add ornamental plasterwork instead of ceiling papers. A ceiling medallion around the overhead light imbues the room with a subtle hint of elegance, while serving as a focal point for the eye. Medallions and other ornaments are manufactured in a wide array of Victorian designs by World of Moulding in Santa Ana, California.

A chandelier really dresses up a traditional bathroom. It need not be elaborate. In fact, the fixture can be rather ordinary in brass or bronze. "A second-rate one that has no particular value would look ridiculous in a formal dining room," says designer Robert Denning. "But in a bathroom it looks terrific." Tom Flemming, a partner in the New York City design firm of Irvine & Flemming, often uses converted gas fixtures from the Victorian era in bathrooms. They come in a variety of styles with globes made of frosted or etched glass and, often, in solid green shades.

Sconces on either side of the bathroom mirror heartily reinforce a traditional theme. They are plentiful with sources located on both sides of the continent—Victorian Lighting Works in State College, Pennsylvania and Nowell's Victorian Lighting in Sausalito, California.

CONTEMPORARY

Because they contrast with the sleek laminates and marble surface treatments of contemporary design, old and new Victorian features in the bathroom have a particularly exciting appeal. For example, modern fixtures can be set in wood frames in a tambour pattern. A new basin can be given a Victorian look when decorated in Victorian motifs and set in a marble vanity. Consider defining a marble tub with wood molding. The molding,

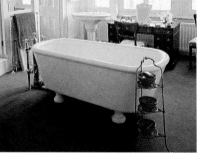

A traditional setting with contemporary ambience. An old tub with its original plumbing hardware takes center stage in this large bathroom. Along the wall are grouped a dressing area and side chair.

Tim Street-Porter/EWA

Jeffrey Weiss

With its sloped ceiling and intricate woodwork, this bathroom is an airy space perfect for grooming and bathing. In one corner, a deep old tub invites the owners to take long soaks.

Gleaming marble finishes make this bathroom, designed by architect Peter Marino, a haven of elegance. The old basin and hardware are surrounded by marble, which is repeated as a chair rail and as the trim on a doorway leading into a separate dressing area.

Norman McGrath

when surrounded with Victorian-style wallpaper, achieves a nineteenth-century look with the tailored "all-of-a-piece" approach favored by contemporary designers. Several types of marble can be used, but the one most reminiscent of Victorian times is white carrera, which is generally incorporated into the design schemes of old-fashioned ice-cream parlors.

In fact, ice cream parlors and other commercial installations are full of flooring ideas for the contemporary bathroom. Ceramic tile floors in patterns of black and white are great, though other combinations are equally appropriate depending on your overall color scheme. New York City designer Ferne Goldberg suggests sand and cornflower blue, beige and pale green, or all black. Besides the classic checkerboard pattern, contrasting stripes and zigzag tile designs also fit into a contemporary setting.

Wallpaper in the Victorian vein can be placed on all walls or limited to a border near the ceiling. The Regatta collection imported from England by Clarence House of New York City is a contemporary paper that captures the Victorian spirit. Leaves form a grid pattern, with tiny flowers in the center, and the ground is beige, while the flowers are blue. Striped wallpaper is also effective because it has the slightly hard-edged look associated with contemporary design. For the Victorian feeling, stripes should be in classic nineteenth-century colors—dark crimson, bottled green, and beige. Usually, matching fabrics are available for shower curtains, enhancing the tailored look of the contemporary bathroom.

Stained, beveled, or etched glass are great window treatments in a contemporary setting. The stained glass is like a prism that floods the room with refracted light and color. For an authentic Victorian flavor, choose a rich amber as the field color with borders in green and blue. Beveled glass adds a sense of richness, while etched windows soften the light without adding color. These two treatments are most effective when the bathroom is already alive with color from patterned shower curtains and floors. Etched glass is extremely architectural looking and draws attention to the molding around windows. Many sources exist for stained, beveled, and etched glass around the country. Some of the most notable are The Beveled Edge in Hoffman Estates, Illinois, The Beveling Studio in Redmond, Washington, Center City Stained Glass of Philadelphia, and craftsman Peter David in Seattle, Washington.

A metal ceiling goes well in a contemporary bathroom. It can be painted in either a contrasting color to stand out architecturally or in a matching color to blend seamlessly with the rest of the room. Tin, nickel-plate, and brass finishes add a touch of luxury in this setting. The most frequently cited sources for metal ceilings are the following: Shanker Steel of Glendale, New York, W.F. Normak

Victorian-era materials are expertly blended in this bathroom. A visually striking tile pattern on the wall sets the background for a toilet with an overhead tank, a double marble vanity, and nineteenth-century light fixture. The complex floor tile pattern reveals a love of decoration.

of Nevada, Missouri, and Entol Industries of Miami, Florida.

Victorian brass wall sconces with etched glass globes beautifully accent modern lighting. Other accessories and details also add Victorian flair to this style bathroom. It may be a small touch, such as a marble doorway saddle or a more noticeable etched glass panel in the bathroom door. The frosting of the etching allows light from the hallway or adjacent rooms to penetrate the space without sacrificing privacy.

Other accessories can be as simple or elaborate as you like. A nineteenth-century mirror can be the only Victorian element in a contemporary bathroom if you prefer. A mirror frame in good condition can be used as is, but if it has a damaged or scratched finish it may need to be stripped. In that case, consider bleaching or pickling the frame to add a contemporary touch to the old. Freestanding towel bars in brass, framed botanical prints and coordinated toothbrush, soap, and toilet tissue holders are other Victorian accessories that will enhance an otherwise antiseptic, white-toned contemporary bathroom.

ROMANTIC AND ECLECTIC

These are the settings in which to indulge your love of fabrics and intricate, even pervasive detailing. With the development of water-resistant fabric finishes, textiles have become an integral part of both the romantic and eclectic decor schemes. Take, for example, shower curtains. Frederick P. Hutchirs and Ronald Whitney-Whyte of Prisma Designs in Los Angeles frequently drape the tub from the center with layers of patterned fabrics. If you use tenting above an old or new tub, they suggest incorporating taffeta, moire, and other fabrics with a highly polished finish. Beautiful brocades in light pastel colors and velvets are other excellent choices, particularly when they are embellished with dressmaker touches such as shirring, contrasting piping, and ruffles.

Designer Joan Barstow of Chestnut Hill, Philadelphia, blends contrasting chintz fabrics for outer and inner layers of the shower curtain. In a bathroom she recently designed, Ms. Barstow chose a chintz with stripes and florals in blue on a pink ground for the outer layer. On the inner layer, she used a coordinating chintz with an allover floral design on a pink ground. Inside this layer, she inserted a plastic liner to protect the decorative curtain. Overhead, she tightly gathered additional fabric with a pink piping border as a valance.

A coordinated shower curtain set from a Victorian-oriented shop such as the Bath & Closet Boutique in Boston is a less expensive alternative. New sets of fabrics for the bath are widely

Visually strong but surprisingly unified, this bathroom has an interesting background formed by the floral-patterned wallpaper, display shelves for ceramic accessories, and a detailed mirror. Though highly decorative, the mirror unit is also practical with its shelves and lighting fixtures that illuminate both sides of the face at once. The vanity is emphasized by dark wainscoting.

The whirlpool tub is a modern amenity but the stained-glass window bespeaks the old in this pleasant, light-filled bathroom.

The stained glass and whirlpool combination is executed slightly differently here. The two are offset by an expanse of contemporary ceramic tile—making up the tub surround and lining the wall. The wall tiles are hand-painted.

available at retail from several companies. Probably the best known is Ex-Cell Home Fashions of New York City. It manufactures several collections, including its "Silhouette" design of swans on a beigy-pink ground. The set includes a shower curtain, vanity skirt, countertop cover, toothbrush holder, soap dispenser, water glass, tissue box, and waste basket. Towels with the matching swan motif are made by Cannon Mills. Ames Industries of New York manufactures an entirely different but appropriate collection called "Mariposa," which includes a lacy shower curtain decorated with flowers, as well as matching towels, soap dispensers, and even vases.

Decorated fixtures add an intricate sense of detailing to eclectic and eclectic-styled bathrooms. Designer Joan Barstow paints or stencils a floral design in pretty pastels on a freestanding tub. She then paints the feet a contrasting color such as pink or pale green. Bathroom tile walls are decorated with stripes painted laterally, and above that, she draws vases brimming with flowers.

In these two schemes, electrical switch plates are often embellished with hand-painted designs, usually floral patterns, while towels are hung on dainty brass hooks widely available at retail.

The entire room can be color-coordinated with pink and blue accents provided by thick luxurious towels. Instead of a tile floor, Ms. Barstow suggests using wall-to-wall carpeting in a soft gray.

Tenting the entire room will conceal deteriorating walls and broken tile in an old house. It also visually softens the room, giving it an air of mystery and luxury. The tent should be gathered around a light fixture in the center of the ceiling and may cover the ceiling only or extend down the walls. Floral chintzes, paisley patterns, and batiks are excellent. You may want to install a decorative metal ceiling or create a coffered effect by applying strips of latticework on the ceiling and painting them a contrasting color.

Walls can be tiled, paneled or left bare with the only Victorian element being a chair rail. At the top of the wall, cornices and crown moldings reinforce the idea of exquisite detailing as do applied moldings beneath the cornice. Moldings and cornices can be painted in contrasting colors or painted to resemble tortoiseshell and marble. For a true touch of luxury, however, have them gold-leafed by an experienced craftsman.

Color schemes can take on a number of Victorian overtones. In

Authentic and romantic, this bathroom has it all—a popular Victorian tile pattern on the floor, an old tub, caned side table, fringed details, and a pleasing abundance of bibelots.

Mike Nicholson/EWA

general, use shades that are opposite each other on the color wheel to achieve the Victorian effect. The main color usually is lighter, with dark tones reserved as accent. Because lighter shades are preferred today, you can freely contrast greens with grays and pinks. Other combinations are green and claret or berry and pale yellow with turqoise accents.

A sense of style and your choice of accessories will unify the disparate elements in the romantic and eclectic schemes. These two decor schemes can absorb displays of Victorian pottery, beaded bags, ceramics and china, and even collections of buttonhooks. Designer Robert J. Melin of Chicago has a collection of old horn beakers, several paintings, old trophies, and a deerhead on display in his bathroom. But that's not all. He has also added

Bill Rothchild

Fabrics are right at home in a romantically inspired bathroom. As shown above, they are used as draperies to conceal the tub. Made exactly as they would be for a window, they consist of side panels, tiebacks, and a deep valance that conceals the shower rod. Used in this manner, the tub is the center of attention. Much thought, too, has been given to the furniture—the side table and the towel rack.

Victorian sculpture, silver serving trays that hold rolled up towels, vases for flowers, a mortar and pestle, tapestries on the wall, and a collection of crystal along one side of the tub. You may also consider adding a stool upholstered with needlepoint, ceramic urns to store bathing sponges, apothecary jars for cotton balls, or other old-fashioned antiques-store finds.

MINIMAL

In a pared-down minimal bathroom, old-fashioned Victorian pedestal sinks and claw-footed bathtubs take on a striking sculptural air. Placed within an otherwise all-white antiseptic-looking environment, the fixtures become a dramatic focal point for the entire space. The visual tension created by the juxtaposition of old and new features can be quite exciting.

White porcelain hardware can be added to white fixtures, or a bit of contrast can be created with brass handles and faucets. Because they are small-scale items, hardware can be more ornate without overwhelming the spare look—gooseneck faucets, for example, with elaborately stamped handles. In an all-white room, porcelain fixtures blend seamlessly into the overall look, while brass stands out and reinforces the fixtures as primary visual elements.

The minimal color scheme is usually monochromatic. Designer Jerry Van Deelen of New York City opts for an all-white background using one-inch ceramic tile on the floor, walls, and ceiling to create an "envelope" that visually frames the fixtures. However, the color scheme need not necessarily be limited to white. Because the spare look inherent in minimalism can be too severe for many peoples' tastes, some designers soften the impact by choosing other colors. Besides white, monochromatic schemes can be devised using pale gray or green, beige, and even pink or blue tile.

Contrasting grouting adds to the visual appeal of the room without detracting from the overall monochromatic feeling. With gray tile, brilliant red or pale pink grouting creates a dramatic sense of contrast, while yellow grouting complements pale green tile. Other suggested combinations are black grouting with beige tile and green grouting with pink or blue tile.

Two-toned color schemes have also gained in popularity among minimalists as a way to soften the industrial style. Within the Victorian color palette, you can combine a soft, antique white tile floor, fixtures, and moldings with pale celadon green walls and ceiling. Or, within that context, paint the ceiling a pale pink and provide matching bath towels.

Floor treatments are another way to add color and a Victorian flavor to a minimal setting. A Greek key design in the center of a tile floor in black or cobalt blue will make an entire room come

Courtesy of Rue de France

A vision of what the minimal bath can be is provided by fabric manufacturer Rue de France in this product publicity shot for its lace products. Though most minimalists eschew soft frilly fabrics, the lace greatly softens the overall effect of the hard-edge design, making this austere design scheme more palatable to many families. The classically inspired window frame incorporates thick crown molding as the top rail.

alive. Add a straight simple border in linear tiles around the edge of the floor. A design painted or stenciled on canvas or plastic matting can double as a practical bathmat.

In large bathrooms, a chaise lounge or an ottoman lends a sense of opulence. Upholster them in solid pastel colors in chintz, silk, damask, or moire. A striking effect can be created by applying black nylon upholstery. "That way," says designer Van Deelen, "the ottoman is very modern and very Victorian all at the same time." Trimmings evocative of the nineteenth century

reinforce the effect. Here, you can indulge with fringe in gold tones or in a shade or two lighter than the upholstery.

Accessories present a problem in the minimal scheme. Ideally, there should be few. The design should include sufficient storage so that toothbrushes, soap, and all the other accoutrements for cleansing and grooming can be tucked away out of sight. However, accessories can be introduced in subdued form. Excellent suggestions include the classic Victorian bowl-and-pitcher set in white, or a wicker bench or baskets to store fluffy white towels.

COUNTRY

Besides the standard Victorian fixtures, a country-style bathroom is the perfect place for one of the old-time toilets with the tank attached to the upper portion of the wall. Manufactured by companies such as Kohler, this type of fixture has an advantage over more conventional toilets. Because the tank is off the floor, the toilet bowl can be placed closer to the wall and, thus, takes up less space. Sometimes it is the only practical choice for a small bathroom. Though the space-savings is only a few inches, it "can make the difference between being able to open the door or not," says New York designer Michael Love.

In a country-style bathroom, you can use the same hardware and fittings as you would in other design schemes, but you can also specify wooden-handled shower heads, spigots, and other wooden bathing accessories that are out of place in other design schemes.

For the walls, small-patterned wallpaper with either geometric designs, or motifs of small flowers like roses or ribbons is entirely at home. Wallpaper borders fit in nicely, too. Stenciling a border that you have designed yourself on the walls is a fun do-it-yourself project. It's an idea suggested by designer Katherine Stephens of Long Island, New York. The technique results in a look that she

Scrubbed pine is at the heart of today's American country look. In this lovely bathroom, it is used in abundance and serves as one of the unifying themes of the overall design. It is also present in the cupboard—an old piece rescued and given a new life—and is used in the vanity. Floor stenciling adds pattern.

describes as "fancifully primitive." Here's how it works: Into a car-wash sponge carve a basic design of a heart or flower. Then dip the sponge into a water-base paint of a color that contrasts with the wall. Apply the sponge to the walls as though it were a rubber stamp. Repeat the procedure to create a straight line of stenciling all the way around the room.

For a more formal atmosphere, apply vinyl wallpaper that is finished to resemble damask. Contrast this with curtains made of fine lace or a polyester "lace."

Though tile flooring looks best in a country setting, you can also install wood floors sealed with polyurethane in oak, fir, and

This interpretation of the country decorating style has definite English overtones created by the architectural bureau. Simpler pieces—mirror, vanity, wall sconces, old towel rack—reinforce the feeling without competing for visual attention.

Pattern proliferates in this bathroom—from the walls to the basin and even to the toilet seat. The hand-painted artwork bespeaks a great attention to detail in a room that is so often considered only in strict utilitarian terms.

even spruce. Leave them natural or apply a light stain that brings out the grain. These also can be pickled by applying white paint that is then wiped off with a soft dry cloth to the desired intensity.

Old gas fixtures that have been electrified give the country-style bath a decidedly Victorian atmosphere. Small wall sconces wired for low-wattage bulbs add a nice subtle touch. Or buy an old pair that has not been electrified and use them as candleholders. Craftspersons such as the famous Ruth Vitow of New York City will design and fabricate custom shades or make them to your designs. Improvisation can be the most fun, however. A large man's handkerchief can hide an existing nondescript shade. Or you can make them from a host of fabrics—a paisley with a neutral ground to filter the light, solid pale pink silk damask, moire, or a combination of gold Chinese silk lined with solid apricot fabric. Simple muslin is just as beautiful and will make the sconces glow. Otherwise, insist upon contemporary fixtures fitted with rheostats that can be brightened for tasks such as bathing and shaving, then dimmed for mood lighting.

Victorian accessories and country decor blend well. Designer Michael Love suggests visiting flea markets for bamboo towel racks and old brass hat racks for hanging towels. Unusual porcelain dishes for soap also abound at flea markets and antiques shops. Look for the type that have a small perforated tray inside on which to lay the soap bar. This enables water to drain down into the bottom of the dish and keeps the soap dry. Available in a wide variety of authentic patterns and colors, they are great collectibles and can be used in other rooms of the house to store pins and needles, thimbles, and even odds and ends in the kitchen.

A thick sheet of clear plastic can be painted with a stencil design, creating an easy-care yet practical bath mat. There's even a place for the old Victorian slop bucket in a country-style bathroom—lined with plastic, it makes a great wastebasket. A wonderful free-standing Victorian screen is ideal for the bathroom. It can be set up to conceal the toilet and lend privacy to a small space.

Large-scale bowls and pitchers add Victorian atmosphere even if they are only used as decoration rather than as everyday items. Place them on an old white iron washstand for maximum visual effect, then add a small checkerboard cloth and an antique dish containing a scented bar of soap.

Color schemes should, of course, complement nearby space whether it is a hallway or bedroom. In a country-style bathroom, creamy white is an excellent choice, as are quiet pastels with contrasting white moldings. However, restrain your application of molding, as it creates a more formal atmosphere that is out of character with a relaxed rural setting.

CHAPTER FOUR

THE LIVING ROOM

◆ ◆ ◆ ◆ ◆

The Victorian parlor was the place where families received and entertained their friends and guests. Because of the public nature of the room, the Victorians lavished great care in its decoration. Generally, they anchored the room visually with an upholstered sofa, supplemented with easy chairs and ottomans. In fact the Victorians popularized upholstered seating with soft cushions that made the parlor one of the most comfortable rooms in the house. To complement the soft furniture, they added chairs with exposed wood frames. Occasional furniture was highly favored and tables were devised for very specific needs. Used for tea, games, and card parties, these tables usually were designed with a pedestal base and often were made of papier-mâché painted with floral sprigs and other naturalistic motifs.

Accessories proliferated during the Victorian Age. Early Victorians often hung a mirror on the chimney and placed burnished gold candlesticks on the fireplace mantel. Genteel Victorian ladies handcrafted needlepoint pillows and made miniature floral bouquets from wax, feathers, and seashells that they displayed under glass domes.

During the middle years of the Victorian Age, the living room became overdecorated. Furniture was ponderous in scale, fussy with detail, and plentiful. The living room was cluttered with folding screens, writing tables, display cabinets for curios, and music stands. Innumerable curios and ornaments like papier-mâché trays and fire

A pleasing blend of traditional and Victorian design, this living room is outlined with wallpaper borders near the ceiling. Simple, elegant, and well-crafted upholstery draws attention to the fluid lines of the beautiful Victorian chairs.

A contemporary setting evokes the Victorian Age with touches including wicker seating, an Oriental rug, and tree-of-life design wallpaper. These are juxtaposed with an Italian lighting fixture, modern art, and a large console table.

A coffee table with the hard, architectural lines of the Japonisme period of the Victorian Age is the center of attention in this contemporary-style living room.

screens decorated with painted scenes of exotic birds and landscapes were added with a heavy hand.

Late in the Victorian era, furniture and interior design reverted back to the spirit of the early years. This reversal was inspired by the importation of Japanese furnishings and the pared-down Oriental approach to decorating. The Aesthetic Movement, a revolt against the overwrought excesses of earlier years, occured at about the same time. These two forces were reflected in Victorian style with the elimination of unnecessary furnishings and the introduction of bamboo pieces as well as Oriental pottery and ceramics.

Furnishings and accessories from all three periods of the Victorian Age are appropriate in modern living rooms. The early and late Victorian phases with their lighter-scaled furniture are easier to incorporate into today's design schemes. But even the floridly designed pieces of the middle period have a place in some room decors. For example, some furniture of the phase looks smashing when upholstered in modern fabrics and placed within a sleek minimal scheme. Used in this manner, it becomes living room sculpture and serves as the center of visual attention.

Authentic Victorian furniture is sold in antiques shops around the country. However, few dealers specialize in the era. Among those with a particular interest in Victorian furniture are Didier Aaron Inc., Margaret B. Caldwell, Mimi Findlay Antiques, Margot Johnson Inc., Kathy Kurland, and H.M. Luther Inc. in New York City. Also, Bob Bahssin in Larchmont, New York, Joan Bogart Antiques in Rockville Center, New York, E.J. Canton in Lutherville, Maryland, Richard and Eileen Dubrow in Bayside, New York, Joy D. Freeman of The Chatelaine Shop in Georgetown, Connecticut, Peter Hill Inc. in East Lempster, New Hampshire, and Richard McGeehan in Bedford Hills, New York.

One of the most faithful collections of reproductions has been introduced by Lewis Mittman Inc. of New York City, a wholesale trade source for designers and architects. This line includes upholstered chairs and chaise lounges as well as sofas that reflect a remarkable fidelity to the originals. In addition, Egyptian-inspired side chairs and armchairs are available through Casa Stradivari in Brooklyn, New York.

As Victorian furniture evolved, so did living room color schemes. In the early period, red was popular, particularly in

Norman McGrath

A simple coat of paint on the walls of this living room draws attention to the ornate ceiling treatment replete with carving and applied molding.

Traditional styling is at its best in this living room. The period furnishings include a folding screen in a tree-of-life design, an ornate mirror, and a sculptural caneback chair on a diamond-patterned carpet.

combination with white accents and gold accessories. By the 1850s, "living rooms were a hodgepodge of lively tones," says Margaret Walsh of the Color Association of the United States in New York City. The color explosion was due in large part to the replacement of soft natural dyes made from plants with those made from chemicals. This new color technology resulted in dyes that were bright and saturated with color. The most popular of these were red, magenta, and a purply pink called Solferino.

Colors softened in later years as the Victorians learned to control the processing of chemical dyes and as the influence of the Aesthetic Movement grew stronger. It is this portion of the long era that is a rich hunting ground for color enthusiasts today. While the Victorian palette retained the dark tones of crimson and Stuart green, it was broadened by craftsmen such as William Morris to include lighter colors such as burnt orange (which the Color Association of the United States forecasts will be a popular choice for home furnishings in 1986 and 1987.) Another shade of late Victorian orange, and one fitting for modern living rooms, looks like what we would call salmon. There is also mauve—which dominated parlor color schemes in the 1890s—and auburn red. Color choices also reflected regional differences. For example, the color palette of San Francisco was much paler and softer than that of the Victorians who lived along the Eastern Seaboard and in England. As a result, when selecting Victorian colors appropriate for today, many designers are guided by those used in the nineteenth-century houses of San Francisco.

Besides colors and furniture, other aspects of Victorian parlors are suitable for modern living rooms:

◆ Trimmings for upholstery and draperies
◆ Trompe l'oeil, glazing, and murals
◆ Needlepoint pillows
◆ Classically inspired bowls and statuary
◆ Parchment, black paper, or silk lamp shades

By choosing one or more of these Victorian elements, you can create an inviting atmosphere in your living room. "The Victorians understood the need for comfort better than anybody else," says interior designer Leah Lenney of Larchmont, New York. "In fact, they invented deeply cushioned seating in the English-speaking world." Before the nineteenth century, sofas and chairs were straight-backed with flat seats and tight upholstery. The loose cushions on many Sheraton, Hepplewhite, and earlier style chairs were added during the nineteenth century. The Victorians also gave us fully upholstered seating such as the Morris and Chesterfield chairs. "Every piece of upholstered furniture that has been made since then has been influenced by that," adds Lenney. "Modern seating has its origins in the Victorian Age."

Garry Burdick

Victorian touches can be subtle yet still stand out in a traditional design scheme as this living room vividly illustrates. Here, the nineteenth-century additions are confined to an ottoman and a patterned rug. They blend well with the classically inspired furniture and wall sconces that flank the fireplace.

SPECIAL EFFECTS

A number of decorative treatments for walls and draperies can add special touches to your living room. Among the most popular types of painted finishes are trompe l'oeil, which literally means "fool the eye," as well as glazing, striating, stippling, and other paint treatments that simulate the look of marble and wood. Finish pieces as simply or as lavishly as you want. In the foyer of interior designer Ann LeConey's New York City apartment, the draperies, shelves, niches, "marble" moldings, and "porcelain" accessories are all illusions painted by artists Karen Becker and David Cohn of New York City and David Polatsek of Harrison, New York. These three artists marbleized the doors and moldings by carefully applying many layers of paint. The walls were glazed, then dragged or striated with steel wool to add texture. Beneath a chair rail, they painted white "molding" and shadow effects on a pale green background that was striated in a half-moon pattern.

Intricate finishes such as these should be applied by a professional painter. However, simpler applications of these techniques can be fun and rewarding do-it-yourself projects. Designer Katherine Stephens of Long Island, New York, has two suggestions for sponging and marbleizing. To sponge a wall, simply apply a color of your choice with a quick-drying water-based paint. After the paint dries, fill a roller pan with white paint or a paler shade of the color you used. Dip a dry car-wash sponge into the paint, blot with a paper towel, and apply the sponge to the wall in a random fashion.

Marbleizing baseboards and moldings requires a few more steps. Paint the surfaces black with a high-gloss, oil-based paint. Using small brushes and red enamel, paint tiny squiggles on top of the black. Repeat this step with gray water-based paint, then dip paper towels in the gray paint and blot the gray squiggles to soften their outlines. Apply another set of squiggles with gold "radiator" paint. Don't concern yourself with being precise, advises the designer. "The more amateurish it looks, the more sophisticated it becomes. You're not after something realistic, but something that is frankly fake."

In addition to the walls, draperies can add a Victorian flavor to your living room. It is in keeping with today's renewed appreciation of detailing to add treatments such as shirring, smocking, and rouching. Full balloon shades, swags, jabots, and side draperies suspended from a rosette are among the more popular drapery treatments reminiscent of the Victorian Age. A soft swag draped over a curtain rod visually defines the window. Usually, swags are combined with jabots and long draperies hanging to the floor. A shirred or tightly gathered valance frames the window at the top and conceals the curtain rod and drapery hardware. A shirred

Chad Slattery

valance can be further decorated with rouching, which is a small frill placed on the top.

There are a myriad of uses for trims, which is a general term for the finishing touches applied to draperies and upholstery. Narrow trims are called gimp, and those that are 1½ inches or wider are known as braid. Both are applied in a contrasting color to upholstery to outline chairs and sofas. Often, they are used in conjunction with fringe. Long bullion fringe can replace skirting on furniture, while a shorter variety, called cut moss, is applied to draperies and table skirts. These treatments look best on full-sized double-hung windows. If your house is like many modern houses with shallow windows, many designers suggest that you

The ornate wall and ceiling treatment in this living room can't help but draw the eye upward. Custom paint patterns and polychrome paint finishes on the crown and ceiling molding blend with a wallpaper border beneath the ceiling to create a riot of color and pattern the Victorians would have loved.

A frilly window treatment sets the tone in this eclectic living-dining area. Colorful fabric in a lovely large-scale floral pattern is draped over the curtain rod in the bay window. On a side window the panels descend all the way to the floor, emphasizing the tall ceilings, and creating an airy atmosphere in an essentially small space.

install wood shutters to achieve an interesting Victorian look.

Because accessories "personalize" a space, they play an important role in almost every living room design scheme. To enhance the plump lavish look of upholstered furniture and to soften the visual impact of chairs with exposed wood frames, add needlepoint pillows from Trevor Potts Antiques of New York City or Mary Darrah of New Hope, Pennsylvania.

Needlepoint is also an upholstery fabric that is an excellent choice for small chairs, benches, and footstools as well as for carpeting, picture frames, curtains and, antimacassars.

In the nineteenth century, needlepoint flourished as a craft for middle-class Victorian ladies, but was also produced commercially in factories by working-class women. Designs and colors varied throughout the period, giving today's collector a staggering variety of patterns from which to choose—small-scaled flowers on light-toned backgrounds from the needlepoint of the 1840s; macaws, parrots, and other tropical birds and huge floral patterns in the 1850s; and subtle geometric patterns such as arabesques, scrolls, and Greek key designs in muted colors from the 1860s. Stitching needlepoint is still an excellent do-it-yourself activity for the home. Sampler kits that include Victorian patterns are available from The Scarlet Letter in New Berlin, Wisconsin, and Alice Maynard Needleworks of New York City. The Scarlet Letter also sells finished samplers.

Courtesy of Motif

In a relaxed version of traditional design, the owners have brought the Victorian spirit into their decorating by specifying a patterned rug for the floor and simple shutters on the windows. The shutters give the owners excellent light control and draw attention to the lovely old window moldings that visually give the room an added sense of volume.

Traditional design can also be stately as this corner of a living room clearly demonstrates. A towering long-case clock visually anchors the space, assisted by a chaise longue in rich brocade upholstery and a nineteenth-century church pew beneath the window. Sparkling wainscoting enhances the Victorian flavor.

Peter Paige.

TRADITIONAL

Soft, "allover" upholstered chairs combined with a sofa with loose cushions unmistakably estabish a Victorian mood in a traditional living room. Particularly appropriate in this setting is a settee juxtaposed with exposed-wood frame chairs and Chesterfield chairs upholstered in damask, satin, velvet, and plain cotton chintz.

When upholstery is embellished with details such as tufting, the indentations of the buttons create small pools of light for wonderful shadow effects. Trims are especially appropriate here. Rope welting applied to the arms and around the bottom of the chairs adds an extra dimension to the seating that will make it a focal point in the room.

Antiques shops often have fine examples of original Victorian center tables as well as occasional tables for games, afternoon tea, and writing. You may want to adapt furniture originally intended for another purpose into a coffee table, or you can take a nineteenth century wood bench and cover it with needlepoint fabric. Because these benches are usually long, they supply more than enough space to set down drinks. And, they won't be damaged if someone in the family insists on putting their feet up on the coffee table. A slab of granite cut to fit the top of the bench infuses the living room with a sense of luxury. Unlike the needlepoint, granite will not stain from water spots on drink glasses and, in a small room, it provides an auxiliary writing surface.

Round ottomans, poufs, and footstools increase seating capacity greatly and add a sense of comfort associated with traditional

Flowery chintz upholstery plays off an Oriental rug in a casual rendition of traditional living-room design. The nineteenth-century light fixture is suspended from a medallion hanging in the center of the room. This classic sense of balance is broken by the liberal use of thick baseboard and crown molding.

Richard S. Mandelkorn

design styling. The Mittman line of reproductions includes an unusual six-sided ottoman completely upholstered in needlepoint. Besides supplying extra seating, this ottoman also will be a topic of after-dinner conversation. If the addition of supplementary furnishings creates too much clutter for your taste, spread them out over several rooms or alternate them in varying combinations for an evolving look.

Lovely old oil lamps that have been wired for electricity and set on tables around the perimeter of the room provide sufficient lighting for reading, games, and conversation. For shades, consider parchment or pretty fabric shades in pleated silk or moire to make the light softer. To combine old and new, place the shades on modern swing-arm lamps extending from the wall. For a traditional room, these fixtures usually look better when they are finished in brass rather than chrome.

Drapery treatments can be sumptuously formal or casual. Although you can have them custom-made, there is a wide selection available at retail that evoke the Victorian spirit at a much lower cost. Karpel Curtain manufactures a collection of "Priscella" draperies that have the look of linen sheers but are actually made of easy-care Dacron polyester. Alive with detailing, these curtains incorporate rouching and sheering and are trimmed with polyester in an embroidery stitch. Other highly detailed curtains for a Victorian living room are manufactured by A.L. Ellis, Milliken & Co., and the Louis Hand Division of Aberdeen Manufacturing. Great Coverups of West Hartford, Connecticut, produces an extensive line of balloon shades. Many larger department stores such as Bloomingdale's and Macy's in New York City import lovely lace draperies made of polyester blends from Europe. Usually, these are sold under the store's own brand name. These draperies are often sold at extremely low prices. Recently, panels measuring fifty-nine inches wide were priced as low as $10.

Because the Victorians manufactured and imported innumerable curios, the choice of accessories is staggering. What you use depends on your own personal taste and budget. There is a wide range of ceramic jars and mementos for every occasion, such as Queen Victoria's jubilee and other royal celebrations. Covered ceramic jars are plentiful and practical—they can hold dainty napkins for drink glasses or hide the key to the liquor cabinet. Boxes made of shell, mother-of-pearl, and papier-mâché make lovely displays, as do collections of Victorian waxed flowers and beadwork. For a truly stunning accessory consider an old-fashioned ceiling fan. Manufacturers such as Moss, Casablanca, and Hunter equip some of their models with fluted, etched-glass light fixtures that illuminate the room while the fan prevents air stagnation and assists the air-conditioning system in the summer.

A sweeping sense of traditional grandeur pervades this bilevel living room that incorporates a music area. Here, an abundance of ornamental woodwork sets a distinctly Victorian tone that is visually reinforced by the Oriental carpets, formal window drapery, and lamp.

Derrick and Love

Rows of skylights and modern casement windows set an indisputably contemporary tone in this living room. Furnishings are mid-Victorian and Oriental rugs.

A soaring ceiling and a dramatic window wall form the perfect contemporary setting for an eclectic mix of rustic and formal Victorian furnishings including prominent and elaborate wall sconces, a table lamp, and diamond-patterned wall tapestry.

Interior windows reminiscent of Victorian Gothic architecture add a slight nineteenth-century sensibility to this unabashedly contemporary setting. Though the touch is subtle, it reflects the powerful pull of Victorian decorative arts a century later.

CONTEMPORARY

Victorian furniture is stunning when juxtaposed with modern classics designed by such twentieth-century legends as Marcel Breuer and Le Corbusier. The fluid lines and mellow woods of nineteenth-century furniture and the spare shapes and austere materials of modern furniture create a stark contrast that is visually exciting. This combination works well when furniture is kept to a minimum, because it assumes the aura of sculpture within the room. Plain solid upholstery and crisp white walls will allow the shapes of the furnishings to dominate the room as they would, for example, in a museum display.

Because Victorian furniture is so strong visually, many designers suggest you select only one large piece—a wildly ornate sofa, for example, decorated with elaborate carving. In this type of room, furnishings tend to look better when upholstered in their original materials. For modern pieces try rich leathers, suedes, or simple canvas, depending on the particular design. Victorian furnishings can be covered with horsehair fabric from Brunschwig & Fils or Old World Weavers, or with damask in solid colors. Besides creating a dramatic setting for classic furniture from two different eras, this combination has practical advantages as well. Interior designer William Diamond of New York City says that it provides an excellent compromise for couples if one likes Victorian furniture and the other prefers modern pieces.

Window treatments can either reflect a hard-edged contemporary approach with narrow slat blinds and solar screens or evoke the Victorian spirit with simple lace panel curtains. Adorn them with short tassels and cut moss fringe if you want a more elaborate look.

Crown, picture, and baseboard moldings will also instill a Victorian feeling in a modern house. Add a chair rail and wainscoting to heighten the mood. For furnishings, try stark modern sofas and chairs against a pale green, salmon, or yellow color scheme. Pink is a true Victorian background color that can be coupled with forest green or contemporary aubergine accents for a striking effect in the living room. You can highlight the molding in modern style by painting it a contrasting shade of white or in a paler shade of the predominant color.

Rich wood floors become the focal point of a room when the boards are stained in alternating light and dark tones. The floor can be further enriched by adding a geometric Arabian pattern needlepoint rug or an Oriental carpet from Bildarian in New York City. Rugs in subtle tones will complement the overall color scheme. Nondescript or cement floors found in many modern houses can be dressed up with gleaming marble or with wall-to-wall carpeting that has a Victorian motif, such as palm leaves and roses in varying shades of red or green. This is often an expensive approach, however, that requires a custom design made by a trade source like Stark Carpet in New York City. Textured straw matting and area rugs are less expensive ways of dressing up drab floors.

If you want your ceiling to be the Victorian element in the living room, apply thin wood strips the length of the ceiling surface. They should be cut six-to-eight-inches wide and spaced the same distance apart. A more elaborate treatment is created by applying the strips in a grid or diamond-shaped pattern. To highlight this embellishment, paint the wood the same color as the walls and the original ceiling the color of the woodwork. This technique works best in a room with ceilings higher than the standard eight feet.

Nineteenth-century accessories add a wonderful old-time flavor to contemporary living rooms. A Victorian wicker or metal plant stand with a large palm or fern immediately establishes an old-fashioned ambience. If the stand is in good shape, leave it in its natural color, but if it has been ravaged by time and weather or has been extensively repaired, paint it a solid color. For other accessories, consider a papier-mâché clock from Marvin Alexander, framed botanical prints from John Rosselli, and antique mirrors from Hyde Park Antiques, all of which are in New York City.

ROMANTIC

"A little too much is just about enough," says interior designer Janet Allen of Plymouth, Massachusetts in describing her strategy for decorating a living room in the romantic manner. This is a great decorating scheme for those who want to live with plenty of soft, plush furnishings and accessories around them.

Anchored visually by a nineteenth-century settee or a modern

Soft balloon shades on the windows, flowery chintz upholstery, and a patterned rug have been combined to strike a romantic note in this beautiful living room. These elements are reinforced by a chaise longue set beneath a window that becomes a quiet place to take an afternoon nap or read in peace away from family noise.

A refurbished Victorian living room becomes the perfect romantic backdrop when furnished with caned and bentwood chairs, bountiful flower arrangements, and an old overhead light fixture.

The essentials of the romantic look—bamboo furniture, pretty chintz fabric, beautiful mirrors, and a folding screen—are in abundance in this room embellished with wall sconces, ornamental woodwork, and high baseboard moldings.

In a former industrial loft, the owner has created an interior landscape framed by an indoor ''window'' that is actually a space divider. A cane-seated chair recalls the luxury of late-Victorian ocean cruises.

Industrially inspired gray on the floors and walls creates an architectural ''envelope'' for a mid-Victorian settee and table. To soften the overall visual impact of the austere setting, a fabric firm, Rue de France, draped the table with lace, which is repeated as the window treatment using a single panel.

reproduction, the romantic living room can absorb quaint under-scaled balloon-back and ballroom chairs. These can be freely mixed with Oriental folding screens, contemporary case goods, and occasional tables. Victorian-style furnishings come alive in a romantic living room when decorated with gilding and upholstered in luxurious brocades, chintzes, and velvets in exciting light colors. The detailing required in such a setting comes from generously applying tassels and other trimmings.

For maximum impact, lace window draperies can be layered with sheers, under-curtains, swags, rouching, and elaborate tiebacks trimmed with embroidery stitching. Though it may sound too ponderous an approach, the lace lightens the effect considerably.

Color schemes in a romantic living room generally are light-toned. The dark burgundies are too heavy-handed. Consider a frosty mint green, pale yellow, or rose instead, using either one of the three for the main background and another one for an accent. If you would rather paper than paint, a monochromatic flocked wallpaper is an excellent choice.

For fabricked walls, try damask or moire. Dyed a light pastel color or antique white, both of these fabrics give walls a wonderful sense of texture. You can also drape these fabrics above the doorways.

Modern houses devoid of interior architectural detailing need not remain that way. Build up baseboard molding by adding an extra layer of wood six to eight inches higher either on top of the existing woodwork or in front of it. Besides adding other details such as picture rails, chair rails, and crown molding, you can also create the illusion of architectural ornamentation with wallpaper. Many wallpaper borders have cornice designs printed on them. Karl Mann Associates in New York City is an excellent resource for ceiling wallpapers that simulate coffering, trompe l'oeil, and plasterwork. These papers come in a number of colorways.

Accessories in a romantic living room can be abundant but should be small in scale to create the slightly cluttered look desirable in this design scheme. Small Oriental ceramic bowls from Limited Editions are great objects to collect and display in this setting. Candles, a basic ingredient of a romantic scheme, can be placed in antique Victorian brass holders and arranged with snuffers nearby. Elegant Victorian mahogany tapers are easily found at many antiques shops. Oil lamps that have been electrified will help in lighting other pieces like Oriental ceramic vases, nineteenth-century paintings or collections of china from antiques outlets such as the Victorian Boutique in Boston. Dismissed by many art historians as a low point in American painting, Victorian-era portraits, still lifes, and landscapes are relatively inexpensive and right at home in a romantic scheme.

In an otherwise eclectic residential loft, the owners have left the pressed-tin ceiling undisturbed. This gives the setting a subtle Victorian reference that is ingeniously juxtaposed with the existing brick wall, new hardwood floors, vertical blinds on the windows, and track lighting.

Jeffrey Weiss

MINIMAL

Though the furnishings for this design scheme are often low-slung stone coffee tables or severely outlined modular seating units, the minimal scheme is actually quite flexible when organized by a sensitive designer. Surprisingly enough, this sort of setting can absorb the wildly excessive furnishings of the middle Victorian Age—grandly overwrought settees and love seats, for example—that do not work in other schemes. Selectivity is the secret to integrating furnishings of any style—including Victorian—into a minimal scheme. For example, one piece of Victorian furniture such as an exaggerated sofa or chair (but not both) can offset a contemporary banquette or other seating unit. The older piece will become the focal point of the room.

Victorian furniture of high quality with exposed wood frames in mahogany or rosewood do not require much work to make them

Peter Paige

Grouped in an unabashedly eclectic manner, the furnishings in this living room range from Victorian chairs, ottomans, and a needlepoint rug to contemporary glass tables, Oriental chests, and a camelback sofa. Tying this pastiche together is the intricate patterned wallpaper, which is repeated as the sofa upholstery.

An eclectic mix of Victorian elements pervades this corner of a renovated living room. A bamboo table set for a chess match awaits the combatants, who will sit on church pews rescued from a Victorian Gothic church.

shine. When using less valuable furniture, however, minimalist designers suggest that a piece be stripped and bleached to lighten it visually and imbue it with a more contemporary spirit.

Upholstery can either blend the furniture into the background or make it stand out even more. Black, brown, or white leather adds a contemporary air to a piece, while mohair is reminiscent of the nineteenth century.

Color schemes can either pull the entire room together or create an interesting diversity. In the classic minimal living room, walls will be pale gray with dark gray carpeting. Although an excellent backdrop for Victorian furnishings, there are other alternatives. Consider enlivening the gray with accents of light yellow, celadon green, or even ice blue. Or reverse the scheme and use one of these accents as the primary color supplemented with touches of gray.

On top of the gray carpeting add a colorful Oriental rug, or eliminate the industrial carpeting in favor of natural wood floors in the palest of tones. A custom Oriental rug in shades of gray hints of Victorian opulence, but can reinforce the no-nonsense minimalist approach to design. If gray is too severe, choose a softer neutral tone such as sand, which is close in coloring to the buff color the Victorians employed in their bathrooms. With bleached floors, a solid sand-colored rug hints at a contrast while softening the room.

For the windows, elaborate drapery with swags, jabots, and long, fringed side panels strikes a slightly contradictory note in a stark industrial-style setting that adds visual interest to the

Philip Ennis

space. In selecting a color for window dressings, minimalist designers usually suggest the primary color of the room or one of the accents. For pure minimalism, however, have the draperies and tiebacks made in varying shades of gray with a long fringe in a slightly paler hue.

Accessories can be simple, like a single nineteenth-century portrait or a large, cut-crystal vase filled with red roses or carnations. Or they can assume classical overtones reminiscent of the neo-Grec phase of the Victorian Age. A shop on New York City's Lower East Side, JerryStyle, sells classically inspired bowls and candlesticks made of copper chemically oxidized to a "Statue-of-Liberty" green. James II Galleries, Ltd., also in New York City, sells elegant antique mirrors.

ECLECTIC

The Victorian Age, with its free mix of widely different styles, was the original eclectic era, says interior designer Peter Kunz of New York City. It comes as no surprise, then, that Victorian and Victorian-inspired furniture and accessories can be woven into an eclectic scheme with little trouble. Scale is the thread that ties the various styles, textures, and colors of this scheme together. Furniture can be from styles hundreds of years apart if they share this common denominator, says Kunz, whose own living room is a visually soothing blend of Victorian and earlier eighteenth-century Georgian furniture.

Noted designer Robert K. Lewis of New York City recommends two different strategies for an eclectic living room. One way is to introduce Victorian pieces in the form of smaller furniture such as occasional tables and ottomans. "People are accustomed to accepting Victorian that way, and these pieces are more easily available on the market," he says. Another is to choose a strikingly imposing Victorian bookcase as the focal point of the room and design the space around that element with contemporary seating.

When selecting upholstery, most eclectic designers suggest you stay with traditional Victorian chintzes, velvets, damasks, moires, and needlepoint, which can be stitched in a raised design creating a three-dimensional quality. To further reinforce the Victorian theme of the living room, add braiding, cording, and other nineteenth-century trims in rich golds or other colors that are in harmony with the upholstery.

For backgrounds, some of the popular painted wall finishes such as glazing, stippling, and wallpapering add a sense of richness to the living room. This can be reinforced by adding imposing moldings such as one-foot-high baseboards that jut 2½ inches into the room from the wall. To add to the eclectic impression, leave highly detailed woodwork in its natural state,

Richard M. Ross

The architectural shell is Victorian, the furnishings modern, the effect eclectic. Soft seating is juxtaposed with beautiful moldings, lace curtains, and a rosette.

Spike Powell/EWA

An intricate Victorian fabric panel be-comes a visually riveting focal point when used as drapery in this eclectic room.

Victorian furnishings set an eclectic tone in this contemporary architectural shell. Atop an Oriental-design rug sit a bentwood rocking and an old nineteenth-century swivel office chair.

Jeffrey Weiss

thus imbuing the walls with the casual air one would expect to find in an informal country house.

Color schemes can run the gamut from light to dark. In the lighter vein that many prefer today, consider pale green, pink, and yellow or a light gray with a touch of blue. However, if you want a dark palette, emerald green and deep red are authentic Victorian colors that adapt quite well to a modern setting when offset with rich creamy accents on the woodwork and trim. According to Robert K. Lewis, the secret to using the dark colors is to choose tones that are rich and reflective. Unlike dull, matte-finished paints, these will not darken the room too much and create an oppressive atmosphere.

Wood floors in good shape can be given Victorian 'flair by marbleizing them so that the wood grain shows through. Floors in extensive need of refinishing can be covered with wall-to-wall carpeting or with a large area rug around which a border has been stenciled onto the floor. In recent department store sales, the prices of Victorian-inspired rugs were low, even reaching the bargain-basement price of $300 for a nine-by-twelve-foot machine-made rug. These are often designed with a center diamond motif of dark green on a pale green ground surrounded with an elaborate border. Hand-made rugs of comparable size, even on sale, will cost at least $600.

Make the lighting as eclectic as you wish. Brass-plated wall lamps from George W. Hansen Inc., and Alsy and table lamps from George Kovacs of New York City can be mixed with tall piano lamps and electrified vases and candlesticks with crisply pleated lamp shades. Or buy an old nineteenth-century vase and candlesticks in a secondhand shop having them custom-wired to meet your lighting requirements. Vases are usually ceramic and may be plain or decorated with a painted floral design. For another custom touch, buy some plain vases and have a local artist decorate them with a portrait of a family member or close friend. These also make lovely gifts for a person who appreciates Victoriana. Candlesticks are generally made of ceramic, brass, or silver. They are sold by The Mediterranean Shop in New York City. Fitted with pleated paisley or black paper lamp shades, they make handsome additions to the fireplace mantel as do antique sconces from Marvin Alexander Inc. in New York.

"Don't be shy" when planning accessories, advises designer Kunz. "The Victorians certainly weren't." Excellent additions in the eclectic setting are classically inspired objects evocative of the neo-Grec phase of the age. Beaded boxes, throw cushions in luxurious solid velvets, and carefully detailed needlepoint are also beautiful. A paisley throw gives a mundane console table a look of sheer elegance. Drape one on a sofa or chair or replace a swag on the windows. Beautiful throws and shawls are available from Diane Love or Vito Giallo in New York City.

COUNTRY

As a design scheme, the country look has two great advantages: First, it is so overwhelmingly popular that country decorating furnishings are readily available. Second, it is such a flexible style, it can accommodate a wide range of interpretations and diverse elements. Adding Victorian flair is one of the big trends today in country decorating. Overstuffed serpentine-shaped sofas with a floral chintz covering evoke the feeling of a Victorian English country house. It is exactly this sort of sofa that has been introduced at retail in this country by Vanguard Furniture of Hickory, North Carolina. Designed for the company by Louis Nichole, the collection also includes an oversized upholstered chair, chaise longue, love seat, and ottoman. To accompany the sofa, a wicker armchair left natural, or painted white or another tone compatible with the color scheme, reinforces the Victorian country look you want.

Wicker furniture is available from a number of sources but one of the best-known is Walters Wicker Garden in New York City, which carries a wide selection of chairs and occasional pieces. If you use wicker elsewhere in the house, you can eliminate it in the

Jeffrey Weiss

Wicker chairs and a wicker table set the country mood in this simple living room beautifully awash with light from a row of mullioned windows.

Courtesy of Laura Ashley

Prettily patterned wallpaper and upholstery imbue this living room with a country air that is visually reinforced by a scrubbed pine chair, hanging cupboard, and old paintings on the wall.

country-style living room in favor of a willow or twig chair, or even one in the Adirondack Style. Twig furniture is surprisingly easy to find. Skilled craftsmen such as Gene Reed of Nyack, New York, will build a piece for you, or one can be purchased at retail from the nearest JCPenney store. Ottomans and footstools upholstered and skirted in a gay floral print provide extra seating while taking up little space, an important factor in a small room. Antique ottomans and footstools are easily found at antiques shops, or you can purchase a new ottoman that is included in the "Open Home" collection by Sears.

Victorian seating easily blends with an antique coffee table made of scrubbed pine, which is a mainstay of the country style. Country auctions and specialty stores such as Kentshire Galleries in New York City are excellent sources for nineteenth-century tables and Victorian pine chests. These chests can double as a coffee table and as an extra storage unit for out-of-season slipcovers and blankets. To complete the Victorian country look in furniture, mix these pieces with modern interpretations of the eighteenth-century wing chair upholstered in the same fabric.

Many fabrics embody a look that is both country and Victorian

Country need not mean Tobacco Road. Here it is rendered in a sophisticated manner using wicker chairs and an ottoman and soft balloon shades in light colors. Bright accent pieces add to the stylishness of this elegant yet comfortable room.

An elegant English-country living room results from the mixing of antique Victorian furniture with extravagant fringe and a lovely needlepoint rug.

Rustic overhead beams and sisal-matting floor covering set the country tone in this living room. For visual excitement, the designers have added floral chintz upholstery and an unusual drapery treatment that freely blends a floral pattern with striped undercurtains at the window.

Bill Rothchild

A sleek rendition of the American country style—twig chairs are set opposite a contemporary Parsons-style sofa with a glass-topped coffee table in-between. An expanse of modern mirroring on the fireplace wall visually expands space and reflects light from the wall sconces around the room. Billowy draperies soften the hard mirror design element.

at the same time. Some of the most extensive collections are produced by Laura Ashley and sold at the company's shop in New York City and in separate boutiques located in larger department stores throughout the country. English in feeling, these fabrics come in a wide selection of patterns, including florals and stripes in numerous colorways. Hallie Greer Inc. of Freedom, New Hampshire, manufactures a floral pattern enlivened with cute little teddy bears as part of the "My Bearable Friends" collection. Available as both a fabric and as a wallpaper, the pattern comes in two colorways—red and green or rose and blue. A nice geometric pattern called "Country Plaid," is sold by Sears in several color combinations. This pattern, too, is manufactured as a wallpaper.

Grid-patterned wallpapers look right at home in a country-style living room. "Kathy Plaid" by Thomas Strahan Wallcovering in Burlington, Massachusetts, and the "Gingham Plaid" pattern sold by Sears are easy to acquire.

A country-style living room is a great setting for special painted wall finishes. Add a chair rail, then wallpaper the upper part of the wall and sponge-paint the lower portion. If you have a wood-burning stove, have an artist paint a trompe l'oeil fireplace mantel on the wall behind it. Detailed with a painted bowl of fruit, candles and brass holders, it can make the stove the focal point of the room.

Creating a relaxed—yet tailored—environment is the key to country decorating. A floor treatment such as wall-to-wall carpeting can tie an entire room together. To make the Victorian elements more prominent in the room, select a muted carpet in a solid gray such as "Tournament II" from Monsanto Textiles of New York City. If you prefer a more casual approach, Hudson Carpet in the Bronx, New York, and many retail outlets across the country sell straw rugs and sisal matting. Painting the floors in a light color coordinated with the overall color scheme is an even simpler method. Protected by polyurethane, the painted surface will last for years.

Window coverings can be equally relaxed. Simple shutters stained or painted a light color may be all that is required in your living room. Roman shades that can be purchased at retail in department stores create a slightly more polished look. You also can sew your own with patterns made by Vogue Butterick Patterns of New York City, available at retail in fabric shops and sewing centers.

Carefully chosen accessories imbue the country-style living room with style and flair. In the Victorian vein there are many to choose from. Lovely pastel-colored wool throws from The American Hand in Westport, Connecticut, and Woolworks in New York City, Portuguese hand-painted plates from The Gazebo in New York, quilted pillows easily found at flea markets, a wicker "root" basket to hold newspapers and magazines from Kayne & Co. in Westport, Connecticut, and white ironstone platters to mount on the wall from Wolfman, Gold & Good in New York are among the more popular items available. Other suggestions for Victorian accessories include majolica plates from Gordon Foster and James II gallery, redware vases from Thos. K. Woodard, and antique magnifying glasses from Philip Priefer, all in New York City.

Bill Rothchild

CHAPTER FIVE

THE DINING ROOM

♦ ♦ ♦ ♦ ♦

The advent of open planning popularized by Frank Lloyd Wright encouraged architects to incorporate the dining room into the living room with, perhaps, a separate eating area included in the kitchen. In older houses and in many custom modern designs, however, the dining room remains a separate and distinct space. In either case— whether you have a formal dining *room* or a casual dining *area*—it can be stylishly decorated in the Victorian manner.

The dining room of a modern house with an open-plan interior needs to be carefully coordinated with the adjacent living area in color scheme, style of furnishings, wall and floor treatments, and upholstery. In a separate dining room, you have more freedom to create a different atmosphere. Even here, however, the design should complement that of the other rooms.

Despite the evolution of some dining room designs, furnishings have changed little in their function since the Victorian Age and can be blended easily into today's dining room schemes. The development of dining room furnishings followed the same course as those for the living room. Early Victorian dining room furniture embodied the light, delicate lines of the regency style. The dining room generally consisted of a round mahogany dining table on a pedestal base and chairs with caned seats. To store

An eclectic riot of materials greets guests in this interesting dining room. Besides the natural-stained wood mantel, the room incorporates intriguing upholstery and imported Oriental accessories that contrast nicely with the elegant table service.

decanters and display china, the Victorians furnished the dining room with a chiffonier, which is a low cupboard, or a sideboard that was larger in scale. Because early Victorian dining rooms sometimes doubled as sitting areas, they frequently were furnished with a pair of ottomans, a settee, and a round mahogany sofa table. Walls were often painted white and accented with red damask draperies hung on a curtain rod suspended from gilded holders.

Dining room furniture in the middle Victorian period became heavier in scale and darker in color. The dining tables assumed new shapes such as oblong, oval, and rectangular. The white walls of earlier years were covered with red-flocked damask wallpaper.

Under the influence of the Japanese and the Aesthetic Movement, a sense of lightness returned to the dining room in the late Victorian Age. Finely scaled furniture was manufactured in walnut and oak, sometimes inlaid with mother-of-pearl. The overall

Luxurious fabrics and details are perfectly at home in today's dining room. Here, a thick rope tieback with a large Victorian tassel keeps window drapery in place, while an exuberantly patterned wallpaper holds the viewer's attention. A nineteenth-century inspired urn displays a bouquet of beautiful flowers to create a particularly pleasing vignette.

shape of the furniture evolved from the lateral and heavier-looking pieces of the middle period to a more vertical form.

Throughout the Victorian Age, the dining room was a nerve center of the house. Though in use all year-round, it truly came to life at Christmas. In fact, our modern concept and celebration of Christmas comes from the Victorians. It is impossible to imagine the holiday without Victorian literary contributions like Charles Dickens's *A Christmas Carol*. To this day, Santa is often portrayed in a thoroughly nineteenth-century manner as a jolly, bearded man driving his team of reindeer through the nighttime sky, seated in a rounded-back sleigh upholstered with red tufted velvet. Our image of the Christmas tree was also born in the nineteenth century. We picture it in our mind's eye as draped with strings of bright red berries or popcorn and embellished with beautiful, fragile, hand-blown ornaments and white candles set on the larger boughs.

Though the Victorians placed the family Christmas tree in the parlor, they often decorated the dining room with a second, smaller tree. Christmas boughs gaily wrapped with bright red ribbon adorned the fireplace mantel while garlands of greenery were hung from the upper molding in front of the windows. Miniature gingerbread houses were baked, then displayed on side tables, while the center table was weighted down with cakes, cookies, and pies.

The Victorian Christmas spirit still flourishes today in Cape May, New Jersey. A seaside resort on the southern shore of the state, Cape May is designated as a historic landmark because of its many vintage Victorian buildings. Each year, the residents of the village hold a Christmas festival with caroling, parades, and visits to historic houses and museums—all decorated in the Victorian style for the season.

You can bring the spirit of a Victorian Christmas into your own house. Set a vine wreath on the front door. Similar wreaths with hand-painted wood angels, baby's breath, and a moiré ribbon are available through mail order from Simple Pleasures of Texas in Angleton, Texas. Although Victorian tree candles have been replaced today by electric lights, Eric's, a shop in Boston, is famous for the Victorian Christmas ornaments it sells. Traditional Christmas decorations as well as wreaths made of moss and flowers also are sold by Faith Mountain in Sperryville, Virginia.

What fireplace mantel is complete without a Christmas stocking and other adornments? Visions of Sugar Plums in Bosworth, Missouri, manufactures stockings in three sizes from pieces of old quilts in velvet, wool, and calico. Or, make your own stockings with a kit from Pieces of Olde in Baltimore, Maryland. Instead of—or in addition to—stockings, embellish the mantel with a replica of Santa's sleigh. Apex International in Boca Raton,

Sandra DosPassos

A corner of the sideboard becomes a still-life. Resting on an antique lace runner is a crackled glass pitcher brimming with lovely flowers. A shell plate holds a potpourri of fragrant blossoms near a delicate bone china cup and saucer.

The abundance of the Victorian Age is aptly reflected in this dining room. A large crystal chandelier adds a touch of glitter, which is reflected throughout the room by deeply cut crystal. Offsetting the glitz are cane-back chairs, a handsome tablecloth, and a tree-of-life–inspired wallpaper.

Randy O'Rourke

Florida, makes a miniature version in natural wicker that looks great on a hutch or side table. A larger sleigh, appropriate as the heart of the dining table centerpiece, is offered by Country Touch of Columbus, Kansas. Small sculpture replicas of the Victorian image of Santa, to display on the mantel or give to a special friend, are sold by High Country Collectibles of Jonesborough, Tennessee. All of these manufacturers offer mail-order services, and some have toll-free numbers to place credit card orders.

There are, however, a number of Victorian design elements that are appropriate for the dining room all year long. These may include:

♦ A round, pedestal dining table in mahogany or oak

♦ Chairs with cane or upholstered seats

♦ Needlepoint rugs

♦ Sideboard for table linens and china

♦ Window swags, jabots, or rosettes

♦ Cut glass and crystal decanters

♦ Antique tea service

♦ A bentwood settee

Regardless of the Victorian motifs you use, the dining room should be designed to meet the needs of the modern American family. In any dining design scheme, the basic requirements are a table to eat at and chairs to sit on. Designer Robert K. Lewis of New York City suggests concentrating on the chairs when you add a Victorian flavor to the room. "In a dining room, it's the chairs that give the space its character," he says. "They form the silhouette, and that's what your eye really reads—their sculptural form. The table is secondary as you read only the surface and whatever is on it." Victorian dining chairs and tables, too, are plentiful and can be found at house sales, flea markets, and even junk shops.

However, if your budget doesn't permit a Victorian table at the moment, you can improvise with a round caterer's table. Designer Leah Lenney of Larchmont, New York, keeps several stored in her garage. When she needs them for large gatherings, she rolls them into the dining room and fits them with pleated skirting to the floor. She places a round piece of plastic cut to fit the top and adds an overlay of lacy Victorian cloth. The tables are sold with four-and five-foot diameters, often for as little as fifty dollars, from a caterer or supplier. In a real pinch, you can ask the lumberyard to cut a round top the size of a bridge table and drape it with fabric to the floor.

Lighting will vary depending on the types of activities the room accommodates. If the space is reserved only for meals, lighting

An inlaid tray is a beautiful backdrop for this detail photograph of an ornate tea service and a folded lace napkin.

Courtesy of Mimi Findlay

Avant-garde? Hardly, this lovely tea service was designed and made in the late nineteenth century. It vividly illustrates the Victorians' talent for thinking ahead of their time.

The Design Council

levels can be lower. When the room is also used for study, reading, or writing, however, illumination levels should be higher. A centrally located chandelier regulated by a rheostat or dimmer allows you to adjust the lighting to the level you desire. Chandeliers designed in the Victorian manner go well in almost any room scheme. Usually, they are made of brass with glass globes or they are made in the Tiffany style with colored or stained-glass shades, but there are many designs and styles in between.

How appropriate chandeliers are for the dining room is debatable among designers. Robert K. Lewis likes them, because they "furnish" the upper part of a dining room. Other designers agree but insist that the chandelier must be high quality—an expensive investment—or the overall look of the room is cheapened. Unless the ceiling is higher than ten feet, placing a chandelier in its center dictates the placement of the dining table directly below. This is a workable solution most of the year, but it will hamper space-planning when you want to use extra tables to entertain larger-than-normal groups for dinner. An alternative is to use wall sconces and lamps placed directly on the dining table.

The dining room is the place in which to indulge in the beautiful table accessories of the Victorian Age. Cut crystal decanters, gleaming polished glass, and pedestal stands in colored glass all add to the Victorian feeling. Also, the visual impact of old silver or silver-plate serving pieces is unforgettable. The Victorians produced a wide range of overscaled dining forks, spoons, and knives that can be used today as serving pieces. Antiques shops, house sales, and flea markets are good sources for these items.

Lace also adds a Victorian atmosphere. Antique lace is often inexpensive and is sold by many shops. Table runners are particularly easy to find, because they were used more infrequently than other linens and, thus, suffered less wear and tear. If antique lace is hard to find in your area, new versions imbued with the Victorian spirit won't be. The continuing interest and application of lace in women's apparel has crossed over into table linens. This is coupled with a renewed desire by consumers for a traditional look for the table, which many manufacturers say can be achieved with lace. At least two table linen houses, Bardwil Industries and Grossman & Weissman, have expanded their lines of lace products to include special Christmas themes, such as poinsettia designs and Currier & Ives scenes.

Richard Chestnut

Who could resist sitting down to dinner at this table? Certainly not anyone who loves traditional styling. With its lace tablecloth and nineteenth-century chairs, this room bespeaks another, gentler era. To complete the look, the owners added a marble-topped sideboard.

Last year Quaker Lace introduced a new line of lace that it plans to expand to more than a dozen different patterns ranging from whimsical to formal. Scranton Lace manufactures a twelve-piece set in the "Wilshire" pattern with flowers in the center surrounded by a solid ground. Several varieties of lace tablecloths that are treated with soil and stain repellent for easy care are produced by Jerhart. Vinyl tablecloths with the look of lace are made in several patterns by Caprice-Geni of KGM Industries, and Ambrose Art Linens offers embroidered linens from the Philippines. All of these products are sold at retail in either department or specialty stores.

These and other Victorian elements can be deftly blended into the dining rooms of the 1980s. Design schemes for each room are reviewed individually below.

TRADITIONAL

"In general, the Victorians were the enemies of anything plain, and so am I," says interior designer Robert Denning. Indeed, "sumptuous" is a fitting description for the traditional dining room, especially one that freely blends the rich fabrics, deeply carved tables and chairs, and abundant bibelots of the Victorian Age.

The traditionally styled dining room revolves around the table and chairs. Armless chairs generally are placed along the sides of the table, while more elaborate host and hostess chairs with arms are positioned at each end. If this approach is too formal for your own taste, surround the table with unmatched Victorian chairs. As a rule, the chairs should be from the same nineteenth-century sub-style—rococo, Renaissance, Aesthetic Movement, for example—but within the sub-styles, they can vary greatly in their individual execution.

A single-patterned fabric uniformly upholstered on the different chairs visually unifies them, while the various frames create an interesting feeling of diversity. For this sort of setting, many designers recommend traditional fabrics—velvets in ribbed, cut, or printed patterns as well as brocades—for a more formal look. Chintz relaxes the atmosphere; long mohair and horsehair give furniture a sleek, sophisticated feeling. In addition, these designers urge that upholstery reflect the colors associated with the Victorian and regency styles, such as stripes in combinations of green and gold or pink and green.

Window treatments should be governed by the room's formality. Full-blown draperies with dramatically draped valances, thick side curtains, rope tiebacks, and an abundance of fringe in velvet or silk are elaborate. A more casual—and less expensive—treatment is to gather fabric tightly on rods placed at the top and the bottom of the window. Lace with delicate borders is in

Marble-topped sideboards come in all configurations and sizes. One of the most frequently found is this variety, which includes drawer space for silverware and serving pieces as well as low storage for plates. The top doubles as a display space for an imported Oriental ceramic plate, flowers, and liqueur decanters.

Wallpapers of the late Victorian Age reflect the considerable influence of the Aesthetic Movement. This paper is the work of craftsman William Morris, who popularized naturalistic designs.

103

keeping with this lighter approach. To vary the effect and allow more natural light to enter the room, place the upper rod halfway down the window, leaving the top half bare.

To establish a Victorian mood immediately, choose wall-to-wall carpeting in a nineteenth-century floral pattern or a geometric pattern such as an Arabian diamond motif. The Palladium II pattern from Mohawk, which is sold at retail, is an unusual design reminiscent of Victorian floorcoverings. Woven in a hexagonal pattern, it includes a range of colors—red, green, and gold—on a cobalt blue ground.

If you carpet other nearby rooms, you may want to change the pace in the dining room. One option is marble either in a uniform color or patterned with alternating black-and-white squares. Another excellent and traditional choice is parquet wood floors. Or simply stencil a parquet pattern on an existing wood floor. This is an especially good way to dress up wood floors that are in less-than-excellent condition.

For lighting, a chandelier with a dimmer combines the sparkle of incandescent light with the flexibility of being able to control the level of illumination in the room. An authentic Victorian brass fixture or one that is Victorian-inspired is the most frequent choice. There are others, however, including billiard lights with green glass globes. New chandeliers designed in the Victorian manner abound at retail outlets. Stifle, a company that makes lighting products sold nationally at retail, has a wide selection of new fixtures that are reproductions or adaptations of Victorian designs. Generally, authentic nineteenth-century chandeliers are sold in antiques shops and through interior designers. Wall sconces arranged in pairs flanking the fireplace or windows add to the Victorian atmosphere. For a softer glow, choose either frosted glass globes or shirred fabric lamp shades made of silk or cotton chintz. Boyd Lighting in San Francisco, a manufacturer of both contemporary and Victorian-styled fixtures, is an excellent source for sconces.

No traditional dining room is complete without table accessories. Lace is the perfect touch here in tablecloths, napkins, place mats, and coasters. Scour flea markets, antiques shops, and house sales for antique silver to use as serving pieces or to put on display. Often, old pieces are embellished with beautiful mother-of-pearl handles that add to their distinctive and exotic appearance. Silver candlesticks can be placed either on the table or sideboard. Throughout the room you can take advantage of the many glass objects of the Victorian Age, such as compotes and cake pedestal stands that will reinforce the nineteenth-century feeling. A palm tree positioned in a corner is a subtle addition, as are nineteenth-century mirrors in frames that are crested or arched at the top.

Traditionalism with a twist: Instead of the regency-striped wallpaper one would expect to find in this room, the designer has surprised guests by specifying an unusual pattern with the soft look of clouds. Victorian-inspired chairs encircle the round dining table, while a folding screen stands at attention in a corner.

Courtesy of Motif

Laura Rosen

What better place to display family photographs than in the dining room? Besides giving them added prominence, it reminds the family at dinner of past good times and brings, symbolically at least, faraway family members home. In this example, the tabletop is flanked by extra dining chairs—beautiful cane-back seating that can easily be pulled up to the table for last-minute dinner guests.

CONTEMPORARY

Here is an excellent opportunity to mix exotic old Victorian chairs with a contemporary table. Rounded-back seating in a variety of upholstery treatments becomes the center of attention when juxtaposed with a glass-topped table on a chrome or brass support stand. A modern Parsons-style table covered with easy-care laminate sets a contemporary tone, as well. Offset this type of table with chairs that either have rounded backs or tall vertical lines. If you have a rectangular table, consider buying an old bentwood settee as seating. It can be placed on one of the longer sides of the table, or recycled into another room as auxiliary seating. Victorian chairs of less than sterling quality are easily imbued with a contemporary spirit—simply strip them and leave the frames natural or apply a paint or lacquer finish.

Designers suggest choosing a contemporary table because it is less likely to be damaged by hot serving dishes. Also, the selection of new tables is greater, which will help in tailoring the table to the size of your dining room. Of course, you may find a round, oblong, or oval Victorian table that you can't resist. Victorian tables will work well with contemporary seating such as modern bentwood or upholstered Parsons chairs.

When selecting upholstery, you have several options. Nineteenth-century chairs can be made true period pieces when they are tufted in velvet or brocade. Or, you can give them a contemporary twist by selecting leather or suede. For a feeling that is both old and new at the same time, trim the leather with piping of the same material in a slightly lighter or darker shade.

Designers generally recommend contemporary window treatments that will not overpower a modern ambience. Selections run from narrow slat blinds in a variety of colors from companies such as Levelor and Bali Blinds to fabric shades that have a backing of solar-sensitive film that reduces heat gain. In the Victorian style, the selection is much narrower—either interior window shutters or simple lace curtains.

Many nineteenth-century-inspired color combinations work well in a contemporary dining room: mint green with red and pink accents; a pastel without an accent color; or a pastel with dark accents, such as pink with hunter green or aubergine. Many contemporary-inclined designers opt for periwinkle blue with cream accents or pale yellow with either dark green or red.

Tie accessories to the overall scheme of the room with color. For example, if you use red as an accent color, repeat it in your accessories by adding a deep red glass bowl. Another tack is to eliminate color altogether in the accessories by using a clear crystal candelabra and glasswork.

Randy O'Rourke

The Victorians' love of the elaborate is seen in this unbelievable floral arrangement placed on a sideboard. To offset the abundance of blossoms, the hostess has added simple candleholders and a woven basket. The poster peeking through the blossoms provides a suitable background.

ECLECTIC

The same principles that govern mixing contemporary and Victorian furnishings can be applied to the eclectic scheme. With this approach, however, you have more leeway to blend widely disparate styles. The traditional circle table can be replaced by an oval shape. These can, in turn, be more ornately decorated with inlaid wood and carving. As in the contemporary scheme, you can mix a modern table with Victorian chairs of the same style; but for a truly eclectic approach, select chairs from several different Victorian periods. The secret to their compatibility may be similar scale or similar materials.

If the chairs you collect do not share either of these characteristics, visually tie them together by upholstering them in the same fabric. Consider picking a modern velvet in a subdued lavender or another light tone. Or select another traditional fabric—chintz—but in a modern hot pink, a vibrant green, or another solid color.

Color schemes, too, can be borrowed from the contemporary palette. But, to be more eclectic, apply colors that are more vivid than traditional hues and a mix of accent colors. The eclectic scheme is supposed to reflect a mistake that works. This requires careful thought to do well, but its advantage is that it gives you a wider range of objects, fabrics, and colors from which to choose.

You may want to create a Victorian atmosphere with accessories rather than color. Nothing achieves this goal like an elaborate centerpiece. In fact, designer Robert K. Lewis suggests that families on a strict budget hold down costs with simple, inexpensive furnishings, so they can splurge on a centerpiece that can be kept on the table all the time. Probably the item most suggested by designers is an exotic epergne, a multilayered nineteenth-century centerpiece on which you can arrange a cascade of flowers or fruit.

Other centerpieces that are frequently sold in antiques shops and at flea markets are made of ceramic and, sometimes, silver, gilt bronze, and crystal. Some are very elaborate, which make them a perfect addition to an eclectic setting. Supplement the centerpiece with a plethora of silver and silver-plate serving pieces from the Victorian Age as well as contemporary and art deco designs.

The eclectic design approach gives you great freedom in selecting window treatments. A profusion of swags, jabots, rosettes, and side curtains in light chintzes or contemporary brocades mixes well with modern tables and chairs. With Victorian furnishings, select modern window treatments such as canvas shades. For a true touch of eclecticism, paint the shades in either a solid color to match the walls or a combination of accent colors used elsewhere in the room. These same shades look striking when

Phillip Ennis

From the floor to the ceiling, this dining room bespeaks the Victorian Age. On the floor is a beautiful needlepoint rug; the ceiling is enlivened with decorative latticework. The hostess has surrounded the dining table with Windsor chairs as a final Victorian fillip.

In the dining room of a restored Victorian house, a nineteenth-century statue doubles as a plant holder. Exquisitely detailed, the statue embodies classical motifs—in its dress and by the water urn in its hand—that heavily influenced the early and late Victorians.

Karl Dietrich-Buhler/EWA

Robert Perron

A simple Victorian pine cabinet stands sentry in a renovated dining room beneath a rustic twig wreath. The hanging light fixture recalls the nineteenth century with its curlicues and opaque shade that makes the light glow.

stenciled in a Victorian floral or geometric design. Shades made of muslin make the window opening glow with softly filtered light during the day yet give it an almost mirrorlike quality at night.

MINIMAL

Bringing Victorian decorative arts into a minimal setting can result in a dining room that is enjoyable as well as functional. In the classic minimal scheme, the walls will be white and the floor covered with industrial gray carpeting, but envision this scene enlivened with a round nineteenth-century table and modern seating. The effect is surprisingly successful.

But don't stop there. Instead of a traditional round table, select one that is oblong or rectangular and finished with an elegant lacquer. For modern seating, choose armless Parsons-style chairs upholstered in canvas or search the antiques shops for high-back Victorian chairs with deep carving.

Another alternative to canvas upholstery is a traditional Victorian brocade, which because of its monochromatic character fits well into a minimal room.

To depart from the classic minimal color scheme, choose an eggshell tone to soften the room or a beige to complement wood floors. If you prefer a dark palette, royal blue or a deep rich plum are Victorian-style alternatives to dark gray, says David Mosson of DM Designs in New York City.

To enliven a gray-carpeted floor, add a needlepoint rug or a flat-woven kilim rug, much like those the Victorians imported en masse from the Middle East. Though antique kilims are expensive and usually too fragile to use on the floor, reproductions can be safely substituted. Generally, these are sold in specialty shops and larger department stores. Because new rugs are much more plentiful, you can shop for just the right one to complement your overall color scheme.

For practicality, add a Victorian breakfront to this setting to store dinnerware. If it is a quality piece, leave it just as it is. Otherwise, strip and refinish the piece leaving it natural, painting it the same color as the walls, or lacquering it the same color as a modern dining table.

A chandelier above the table helps to evoke Victorian nostalgia without interfering in the overall minimal concept. A round chandelier will echo the lines of a similarly shaped table. If your table is rectangular, an old billiards fixture will add a nice touch. These are long and narrow with etched glass globes at each end and are usually found in antiques shops. For supplementary illumination, place uplight fixtures in the corners so that they wash the walls or highlight a painting.

Though backgrounds in a minimal setting are usually treated so that they will recede visually, they need not be dull. Designer David Mosson suggests upholstering the walls with velvet as a subtle reference to the Victorian Age restated in a completely contemporary manner. A more practical alternative, he adds, is to specify ultra-suede instead of velvet. While honoring the spirit of the minimal design approach, this sort of wall treatment adds softness and gives the walls a striking luster.

Window treatments such as an elegant black silk swag and simple side draperies follow the Victorian tradition, or, as many contemporary designers suggest, place brass rods at the bottom and two-thirds up the frame, and cover the rods with tightly shirred fabric. A gray silk will echo similarly colored walls, while simple muslin or crepe will complement a beige color scheme.

Rotating accessories is a simple yet effective way to keep a room looking fresh and different. On the breakfront you may want to place an exuberantly designed silver tea service from the middle Victorian period. Then, as the seasons change, replace the tea service with colorful nineteenth-century Oriental ceramic plates. For maximum visual effect, set the plates on small wood or lucite stands and highlight them with low-wattage downlights recessed in the ceiling or hung from a track fixture.

ROMANTIC

Many of the decorative elements used in a traditionally designed dining room are equally at home in a romantic setting. The primary difference is that in a romantic scheme, colors are much softer. There is, also, the opportunity to incorporate a greater number and variety of accessories that

The Victorians' love of craftsmanship is seen in this collection of pitchers and a teapot. The highly detailed design is exacting, yet subdued, creating an enticing sense of contradiction that adds to the interest of the individual pieces. The fluid lines are also appealing.

Ornate silverware, floral-patterned table service, and glittering crystal set a tone of opulence so dear to the Victorians' heart on this sophisticatedly decorated table. The deep relief of the champagne bucket recalls the late Victorian silversmithery and complements the lovely cut crystal vase.

give the romantic room a unique flavor. Because Georgian and Victorian furniture blend so well, this is an excellent combination for the romantic dining room. If your budget allows, select authentic Queen Anne chairs; if not, many fine reproductions are sold at retail. Group these chairs around a plain-lined Victorian country table. Rounded-back chairs upholstered in modern leather can be substituted just as easily. These same chairs also look exciting when paired with the more rectilinear bamboo and faux-bamboo tables.

In a large room, you can create a separate sitting area in one corner of the room, providing a restful place to enjoy before- or after-dinner drinks or the Sunday paper on a lazy afternoon. Change the pace here if other furnishings in the room are Victorian by installing contemporary banquette seating. Or, furnish the corner with a Victorian bentwood settee or voluptuous

chaise longue. Select a small papier-mâché table to set down drinks or a small table lamp with a pleated moire shade.

If the dining table is to stay in place all year long, a chandelier is an excellent choice for general lighting. If, however, you supplement the center table with additional smaller tables for larger gatherings on holidays and other family occasions, you may want to put lamps with frosted glass shades directly on the dining table. Then add wall sconces or even a classically inspired torchere in each corner of the room. A candelabra that can remain in place on the table is an excellent choice and forms the anchor for a centerpiece.

Because the color scheme sets the overall tone of the room, much thought should be given to its selection. Designers often recommend a light scheme in a room enlivened with accessories, fabrics, and furniture, because dark backgrounds tend to make the setting oppressive. Janet Allen, an interior designer living in Plymouth, Massachusetts, who is well known for her soothing, romantically spirited rooms, suggests a pale rose. Evocative of the Victorian Age, this shade is flattering to guests and easy on the eye. As a background color, rose will encourage guests to linger around the table for lively after-dinner conversation that cements new friendships and strengthens old ones. Or lighten the rose tone with white until it is the merest blush of color, much like facial make-up. Applied uniformly to the walls and woodwork, this color selection makes the boundaries of the room recede so that a small room seems much larger. As alternatives, consider a very pale yellow or a light pastel hue of a dark Victorian color— gray, royal blue, or burgundy.

Of course, you need not rely on paint alone. Wallpapers in reproduction Victorian patterns or in designs and colors that evoke the nineteenth century are rapidly becoming available in greater numbers. These can set the tone you want when used alone. Embellished with wainscoting, however, they make a strong Victorian statement.

Another wall treatment favored by many designers is fabric. For a sleek, sophisticated look place it directly on the wall. Draping the fabric on long rods spanning the length and width of the room is a more exotic approach, and one that hides walls that are in less-than-sterling condition. The effect is quite striking and is a strategy commonly adopted by families living for a short term in rental houses or by those who need additional buffering from noise.

Nothing sets a romantic tone like brocade silk draperies hung over the window beneath a dramatically draped swag. If you have sufficient privacy from the view of passersby and neighbors, use a swag by itself. Pretty lace sheers behind the draperies will add to the romantic look. Or eliminate the draperies and allow the

Tucked in a sunny corner, this intimate dining area is imbued with the delicacy of the nineteenth century, a quality all-too-often forgotten amid its admitted excesses. Coordinated fabrics on the windows and table set a frilly mood that is heightened by the stoneware pitcher, flowers, and lacy overcloth.

The Victorian influence in decorating today can be pervasive and subtle at the same time. For example, in an architecturally splendid dining room, a simple rectangular table is surrounded by curved Windsor chairs. The atmosphere is furthered by a needlepoint-design rug and a gleaming chandelier.

Peter Paige

Subtle, soft illumination that is eminently Victorian in spirit is provided by this lovely etched-glass wall sconce. The exuberantly designed holder is in the shape of naturalistic motifs similar to those on the wallpaper. Sconces are available at flea markets and in reproduction from many retail lighting outlets.

sheers to hang by themselves to bring more daylight into the room. Gauze is a frequently overlooked material that can establish a dreamlike mood in a dining room when draped in profusion over a gilded curtain rod and allowed to fall in gentle folds to the floor.

Or dispense with draperies altogether. Dainty etched glass with a floral or other naturalistic design causes the windows to glow when struck by sunlight yet protects your privacy. To avoid the "big black hole" appearance that windows can have at night, obscure them with standing screens that can be removed during the day. Screens can be valuable antiques or simple wood panels hinged together and painted a solid color or upholstered with fabric. One unusual but beautiful application of this idea is relatively inexpensive: Buy two hollow-core doors at a lumberyard, hinge them together, and paint them a solid color. For a twist that will have your guests studying these screens all evening long, ask an artist to paint them with a trompe l'oeil scene. The blend of this elegant surface treatment and a simple—and very inexpensive—material is visually stunning.

COUNTRY

Because this design scheme is so versatile, it can accommodate several types of furnishings. Probably the first that comes to mind is a beautiful old table in golden oak surrounded with high-backed chairs upholstered in leather or needlepoint. A marble-topped sideboard, though expensive, is a perfect complement.

Several varieties of chairs are appropriate. Wicker is inherently country and Victorian at the same time. For a touch of romance in the country, fit them with loose cushions tied to the frame with lacy ribbons. Wicker can be treated to suit your taste. Pieces in good condition can be left natural and simply varnished to seal the wood and caning. If you want to paint the chairs, choose a contemporary white or repeat the color of the walls. Then upholster them in a relaxed country fabric such as Hinson & Company's "Joanna" print or "Dorothy" lattice patterns. Both are manufactured in several colorways, including blue-and-white and red-and-white.

Bentwood café chairs also fit naturally in this setting, as do willow or twig furniture for a more rustic atmosphere. For storage, a glass-front cabinet can be incorporated into the scheme with or without a sideboard. In a large room, create a second seating area with a cane-seat bentwood settee and an old mahogany office swivel chair.

In a country setting, shutters are a natural choice for window treatments. Simple drapery, such as café curtains, also blends well into this scene. The simplest way to cover the window, however, is to buy a shade and embellish it with a big tassel that echoes the accent color of the room.

Color schemes can range from parlor mauve with accents of green and white to a solid green or a relaxing combination of rose and cream. Cream accents also mix well with light blue as well as pale yellow. For a true country touch, however, take a hint from Huck Finn and whitewash the walls. Applying textured paint will add a rustic touch. Usually, this is regular latex paint to which sand has been added. A rougher texture is created by many designers who replace the sand with kitty litter. Paneling imbues the country dining room with a cabinlike atmosphere. When using paneling, apply it all the way to the ceiling and eliminate all moldings except for the baseboard.

A tin ceiling is an authentic Victorian application that also creates an exciting country look. You can also apply wallpaper on the ceiling with or without borders in color blends of white on a ground of blue, green, or yellow. Dining room rafters are easily given a country air when they are painted in contrasting colors from the Victorian palette. Wood floors can be left plain or decorated with needlepoint carpets and rag rugs.

Accessories for the country setting are fun to choose. Flea markets and antiques shops usually are well stocked with plates that you can stack on the sideboard. For added detailing, separate each plate with a white doily. Pedestal cake plates and compote dishes can be displayed in a glass-front cabinet or right on the table. To soften these visually, add woven baskets in the room and, when company comes, fill them with wild flowers.

CHAPTER SIX

THE BEDROOM

♦ ♦ ♦ ♦ ♦

Bedroom furniture from the Victorian Age is plentiful—and practical—for today. Though a big four-poster or brass bed comes immediately to mind, there are many other Victorian furnishings and accessories appropriate for a modern bedroom. They include:

- ♦ Large wardrobes or armoires
- ♦ Dressing tables
- ♦ Full-length mirrors
- ♦ Occasional chairs
- ♦ Washstands topped with marble or faux-marble
- ♦ Bedside cupboards
- ♦ Quilted satin bedcovers or patchwork quilts
- ♦ Perfume bottles and framed photographs

Because of their utilitarian nature, changes in bedroom furnishings were dictated more by fashion than technology during the Victorian Age. In both the early and late portions of the era, the bed usually was a four-poster draped to the floor with wool curtains that were drawn at night to conserve warmth. The half-tester bed became

Attaining the Victorian ideal of coziness, this bedroom has it all—a nineteenth-century-inspired four-poster bed, lovely chintz fabrics, and multilayered bed dressings. The fireplace is bedecked with hand-painted tiles.

popular in the middle part of the Victorian Age. It included a canopy with short curtains overhead to insulate the sleeper's head and shoulders from cold. Both kinds of beds usually were constructed of deeply carved mahogany, rosewood, or walnut.

Metal beds fabricated from iron or brass became fashionable during the last years of the era. These beds had a delicate and airy look befitting the last years of the Victorian Age. Many of the iron beds were embellished with curlicues, while those made of brass usually had curved or rectangular headboards and footboards.

To supplement the bed, the Victorians furnished their sleeping quarters with a four-drawer chest of drawers, which remained essentially the same, in design terms, throughout the era. Wardrobes, or armoires as we more frequently call them today, began as simple, if gargantuan, storage units used in lieu of closets. In the middle years of the era, they evolved into floridly decorated pieces sometimes inlaid with mother-of-pearl in intricate floral patterns.

To complete their bedroom furnishings, the Victorians added a dressing table, desk, bedside tables, and seating. The dressing table had one or two drawers, as well as a mirror in a stand that was shaped in either a heart or rectangular design. Sometimes, Victorian bedrooms incorporated a davenport, which is a small desk with a slanted writing surface and a chest of drawers. Almost always, the bedroom had a mahogany bedside cupboard, often designed with a serpentine front, to hold the chamber pot. Seating generally consisted of a small sofa, chaise longue, and/or occasional chairs. Though the designs of these pieces followed the evolution of living room furniture, they remained simpler and often were painted rather than upholstered.

Bedcovers varied greatly depending on the region. In affluent urban areas, covers were often quilted satin or crocheted, decorated with long fringe, while country bedcovers were a riot of colorful patchwork quilts.

Depending on their individual condition, design quality, and size, any of these furnishings are appropriate for today's bed-

Like the designer of this bedroom, the Victorians loved a plethora of patterns. Here, they enliven the walls, are used in the bed canopy, and have become beautiful draperies in a restful traditional setting.

Careful groupings of patterns creates an entirely different look in this romantic bedroom. Fabric curtains on the four-poster bed can be drawn at night for privacy and additional warmth. Crinkly bed dressings are soft and inviting. The scalloped heading at the top of the bed hints of the great care that was taken in planning the design of the bedroom.

A delicately designed iron bed visually anchors a country-style bedroom that includes the essentials of this look—wicker furniture and lots of throw pillows.

What better place for an intimate breakfast than in bed? For complete comfort, the designer of this room has included a bevy of bed pillows with lace detailing beneath a frilly canopy. The lace trim is repeated on the elaborate window drapery.

room. Of course, the most important element in the bedroom is the bed, which should, it goes without saying, have a modern mattress and box springs to ensure comfort. If you buy a four-poster bed, follow the lead of the Victorians and apply a fabric canopy and curtains. The drapery will drown out distracting noises that may keep you awake. To add an extra sense of detailing, specify one fabric for the outside of the canopy and curtains and a second, quieter pattern for the interior lining.

Only slightly less important than the bed in a modern bedroom are the backgrounds and window treatments. Walls should be painted in soft colors or papered with a small pattern. Avoid busy patterns and bright, bold colors, because these stimulate, rather than relax, the senses. As for flooring, carpets or rugs are generally preferable to bare wood, tile, or marble, which are more of a jolt to your feet if you get up during the night and when you step down from the bed in the morning.

Window draperies can be designed in the Victorian manner, then modified to keep light from the sun or from the headlights of passing cars from penetrating the room. The lining can be cotton that is either plain or coated with fiberglass, or a material that has been aluminized. Sew one of these onto the back of the drapery material or between the curtain and the lining to conceal it from view.

Bedroom furnishings in the Victorian vein are widely available. Antique pieces most frequently are sold by dealers and interior designers as well as at country auctions and, sometimes, at flea markets and house sales. Fortunately, a number of new bedroom products, particularly beds, are manufactured in the Victorian style and sold at retail. Among the nationally known brass and iron bed manufacturers are J/B Ross, Brass Bed Company of America and its Iron Classics Division, Dresher, Swan Brass Beds, Berkshire, Corsican, Benica Foundry & Iron Works, and Baldwin Brass. These companies make beds in a variety of styles from Victorian to contemporary. Design Innovations of Woodbury, New York, and San Francisco manufactures a beautiful Victorian daybed that combines iron and brass. The bed has a hidden trundle that rolls out and pops up to sleep two persons comfortably. A handmade brass "Sleigh" bed is available from Charles P. Rogers of New York City. Lisa Victoria Brass Beds of Petersburg, Virginia, specializes in Victorian style metal beds. Additional sources include Robert Brass Company of New Milford, Connecticut, and A Brass Bed Shoppe of Cleveland Heights, Ohio.

For other reproduction furnishings look to London Antique Dealers of San Diego, California, which sells a replica of a Victorian pitcher-and-bowl stand in walnut with barley-twist turned legs. Magnolia Hall of Atlanta sells via mail order hard-carved reproduction Victorian sofas, chairs, tables, lamps,

A huge bureau sets a Victorian tone in this bedroom, ably assisted by the patterned wallpaper and a typically nineteenth-century window treatment—a ruffled side drapery that preserves privacy from street view but allows natural light to gently filter into the room.

In this cozy bedroom corner, the side drapery almost becomes an architectural element as it echoes the angle of the sloped ceiling. To furnish the corner, designer Georgina Fairholme chose a Victorian slipper chair with button tufting and a wicker stand displaying an assortment of accessories.

A delicately scaled iron bed and a bountiful selection of wicker furniture create a romantic atmosphere in this bedroom. The diverse materials are unified through the use of a pale color scheme with blue accents in the bed quilt and chair cushion.

Keith Scott Morton

clocks, and mirrors. An upholstered petite love seat on a mahogany frame and other reproduction Victorian furnishings for other rooms are available from Martha M. House of Montgomery, Alabama.

Bed dressings evocative of the nineteenth century are plentiful at retail, too. Jerhart of Chicago makes embroidered eyelet comforters as well as bed ruffles, pillow shams, and sheets. Designers Yale and Frances Forman have grouped many different styles, including Victorian, into their "American Legacy" collection of fabrics, wallcoverings, and lamps. Oxford Drapery offers a quilted bedspread with lacy side panels and matching curtains, while Lorraine Linens manufactures lavish, all-lace bedspreads. Avante makes a ruffled bedspread with coordinating pillow shams, draperies, and a table skirt. Bill Blass has designed a beautiful bed ensemble for Springmaid called the "Windmere" collection with dusty pink rosebuds on a taupe background. "Windmere" includes sheets, pillow cases, a comforter, bed ruffle, and shams.

"Meadow Mauve" by Marimekko for Dan River is a sheet pattern of delicate white flowers on a rich mauve background. "Camille" by Utica for J.P. Stevens is a collection of sheets with ruffled hems, lace borders, and contrasting piping on the pillowcases. The pattern is of pink flowers on a sea-foam green background. A comforter, bed ruffle, and shams are also included in the collection.

Beautifully ruffled, decorative pillows are available from Brentwood in solid fabrics as well as from Mirafoam and Riverdale in floral prints. Martex makes the "Tremont" pillow, which is a floral design on a bone moire ground with a contrasting ruffle.

For drapery fabrics, Oxford Drapery offers beautiful knit panels resembling lace while Gilcreast has an open-weave ensemble with

An assortment of patterns creates a comfortable background for the Victorian furnishings in this bedroom. Beginning with the needlepoint-design rug, the room incorporates a slipper chair, tall standing mirror, and a dark-stained bureau.

Against a sea of soft blues, a wicker dressing table and chair create a quiet oasis to read or catch up on correspondence. The simplicity of the setting is enlivened by richly ruffled draperies and a Victorian birdcage in the background.

Keith Scott Morton

A sculptural brass bed is the center of attention in this lovely country-style bedroom. Fitted with ruffled bed dressings, it is flanked by old prints at one end and a nineteenth-century trunk at the other. A wicker chair and floral-patterned draperies reinforce the casual rustic mood of the room.

This room evokes a different sort of Victorian feeling. At the center is a massively scaled bed illuminated at night by gooseneck reading lamps attached to the wall. To the side, an old rack holds towels, while against the side wall is a small mirror and nightstand.

A still-life photograph reveals the delicate beauty of Victorian fabrics. Here, beautiful lace is artfully draped around old slippers and gloves on a stylishly cluttered dressing table.

Accessories can be a key in adding Victorian flair to your home. In this setting, the nineteenth-century elements are the breakfast table linens, including a napkin and tea cozy. They are arranged on a bed covered with a quilted spread and ruffled pillow.

lace panels, tiebacks, and undercurtains. Aberdeen makes several varieties of ruffled curtains as well as florals. Jean Roberts manufactures calico curtains with tiebacks in the form of bow ties, valances, and ruffles. Three prints by Raintree Designs are perfect for draperies and can be mixed to create a coordinated, tailored look. They are "Faery Lights," "Forget-Me-Nots," and "Glory Roses." These and other Victorian design elements can be deftly woven into today's bedroom schemes.

TRADITIONAL

"Although the Victorian Age was basically considered a tasteless era, it's a wonderful period to draw from," says interior designer Gary Zarr of New York City. "Used in refinement and with restriction, it has marvelous curves and shapes that go well with traditional furniture."

Most bedrooms in the traditional vein are anchored by a four-poster or canopy bed, which sets the overall tone of the room. To bring in a Victorian flavor, Zarr and other traditionally inclined designers recommend adding a large faux-bamboo armoire with carved finials. Besides adding practical storage space, the armoire brings to the design scheme a hint of the late Victorian Age when the Japanese influence was at its height. A chest of drawers and a desk drawn from the early Victorian period provide additional storage. These furnishings reflect the light and delicate lines of the preceding regency style.

A collapsible table made of bamboo or faux-bamboo makes an excellent side table for an occasional chair. It's large enough to support a lamp, ashtray, and other accessories with sufficient room left over to keep a book handy for late-night reading.

Victorian chintzes, particularly those that simulate the look of striped moire silk, add a sophisticated tone to the upholstered furniture. Choose colors that complement the overall color scheme. In making your selection, investigate light pastel versions of the dark Victorian palette—pinks, blues, sea green, and beige.

These colors are also suitable for other backgrounds in the bedroom. If you prefer wallpaper, there are several patterns available that simulate damask fabric sold by Brunschwig & Fils. This company, as well as Clarence House and Louis Bowen, offer wallpapers that make the walls appear stippled, mottled, or glazed at a much lower cost than these special finishes. The papers can rise unimpeded to the ceiling or be combined with wallpaper borders from Rose Cumming or Cowtan & Tout that are decorated with patterns of dentils, swags, and jabots.

A custom look can be created with varied ceiling treatments. Repeat a color in your wallpaper pattern as the ceiling color or blend complementary, relaxing tones. Instead of the harsh white used on many ceilings, select what designers call "photographer's white," which is a shade devoid of all color. It can be combined with any wall treatment. Or follow an old New England tradition and paint the ceiling sky blue, which goes beautifully with walls painted a soft beige or sand color.

Because many people want the floor to be soft when touched by bare feet, wall-to-wall carpeting is a frequent choice as a floor-covering. Atop that you may want to place area rugs such as a large Oriental carpet or needlepoint rug to evoke a Victorian mood. If you eliminate fitted carpeting in favor of area rugs, stencil a border around them in a Victorian floral or geometric motif.

Window treatments can be elaborate in this setting. Many include large, elegant valances and smock headings dripping with fringe. Fabric-wrapped curtain rods and crystal finials with ceramic rosettes embedded in the center are simpler treatments that can be just as beautiful and as detailed. The drapery fabric can be repeated in the lamp shades, which may have gathered ruffles at the top and bottom. A "soutache," or an underpiping that resembles upholstery welting can peer ever so slightly beyond the ruffle. This is a particularly effective touch of detailing when the soutache is of a contrasting color from the lamp shade.

Lamps in a vaselike shape are widely sold at lighting and department stores, or you may find exactly the lamp base you want in the form of a vase at an antiques shop. A lighting shop can wire an older vase for electricity and fit the top with a lampholder. Swing-arm lamps from a source such as Paul M. Jones also do well in a traditional setting. Several in the Jones's line are made of gunmetal and brass.

CONTEMPORARY

Although this sort of room usually has a modern bed, it can be given Victorian zest by adding a padded backrest upholstered in a quaint, light-colored chintz. Repeat this fabric selection on the bedcovers and pillows, but update it with channeling, padding, and other modern treatments. You can also drape a decorative mohair throw atop the bedspread or fold a quilt at the foot of the bed.

Because many contemporary bedrooms have built-in cabinetry, your opportunity to incorporate other Victorian furniture is usually limited to seating. Rise to the challenge by selecting an ornate wicker chair, or a reproduction chaise longue with an

In the sitting area of a traditionally styled bedroom, a horsehair sofa awaits the owner for an evening of reading or visiting with friends. This unmistakable Victorian element is paired with a round-back chair, table, and a detailed window treatment.

The opulence of traditional decorating is enhanced by a profusion of bedcovers embellished with wide ruffles. This touch of Victoriana visually softens the room, adding to its feeling of welcome.

Phillip Ennis

To establish a nineteenth-century atmosphere, the designers at McMillen, Inc., of New York City, visually anchored this room with a delicately scaled iron bed.

Keith Scott Morton

When draped artfully, windows can become a focal point of a room. In this bedroom the owner has utilized side draperies, a ruffled valance, and undercurtains in lace for a soft Victorian touch.

Sam Sweezy

The Victorian spirit assumes a more austere look in this setting. The four-poster bed has been left unadorned with fabric, as have the contemporary windows.

Bill Rothchild

White wainscoting and a contemporary floral wallpaper with a nineteenth-century feeling set the mood in this visually soft and inviting child's room. The Victorian accessories—a gabled-roof dollhouse and a miniature gazebo with lots of gingerbread—are prominent. A subdued color scheme in shades of lavender completes the look.

exposed wood frame that can be upholstered in a fabric that blends with the color scheme of the walls or bedding.

If you find a wonderful old upholstered chair and ottoman, outline them in a solid color welting and add long fringe around the bottom of the frame that repeats the overall color scheme. Other seating, such as a modern built-in banquette, may already exist in the room. To blend this element into the design scheme, upholster it with fabric that repeats the pattern or color of the bed dressings. One piece of furniture you definitely will need is a bedside table. An old Victorian cupboard is good for storing nighttime essentials, for keeping the telephone within reach, and for setting down that first cup of coffee in the morning.

Hardware such as brass knobs and hinges is an easy way to blend an old cupboard with contemporary built-in storage. This is a small touch, that is effective for mixing disparate design elements and reflecting an attention to detail. If the cabinetry has a decorative wood pattern, repeat it as wainscoting on the walls, and add other architectural elements such as picture moldings and chair railings.

Contemporary color schemes in the bedroom are generally light-toned. Select closely related shades for the woodwork. A comfortable, soothing cream, sea-foam green, pale blue, or rose makes a good backdrop for restful sleep.

Recessed lighting is almost *de rigueur* in a contemporary scheme. While this provides efficient overall illumination, you also will need task lighting in a sewing or reading corner. A Victorian table lamp is an excellent choice that is practical and reinforces the Victorian mood. Wall sconces add an air of sophistication and make the walls glow with their reflected light.

Accessories will be fun to select. Find an old dilapidated Victorian column and saw off the capital, or top, and use it as a low side table next to a chair or chaise longue. A large ceramic vase, can be made the center of attention by placing it atop low cabinetry under a window. If you have a fireplace, equip it with brass andirons and place complementary candlesticks on the mantel. Vases brimming with flowers look wonderful on the bedside cupboard and enable you to awaken to their fresh clean scent in the morning. A large ceramic bowl in a severe white assumes the look of sculpture when it is piled high with colorful fresh fruit.

ECLECTIC

With its exciting mix of opposites, the eclectic bedroom is a great setting for a Victorian brass bed covered with lacy bedcovers and antique quilts. The effect is even more striking when the bed is flanked with avant-garde accessories atop contemporary lacquer tables.

You can take the opposite approach, too, and choose a reproduction Georgian four-poster bed and bring in bedside tables and other occasional furniture as the Victorian elements. Perhaps a Victorian settee or small sofa is more to your liking? In that case, upholster it with a modern reproduction of a nineteenth-century fabric with exciting trimmings like bouillon fringe in either a rich Victorian gold or a soft contemporary color.

Peter Paige

A four-poster bed is elegantly draped with gauzelike lace. This demure fabric is offset by a classically inspired secretary, creating an understated eclectic bedroom that is exciting to view but not too stimulating for a restful night's sleep.

Keith Scott Morton

Fanciful in the extreme, this heavily carved Victorian bed is a craftsman's dream. From the overwrought headboard to the only slightly-more-subdued spindles at the foot, this bed instantly creates an eclectic design scheme regardless of the furniture with which it is paired.

Offset this homage to the past with a new Parsons-style table covered with plastic laminate in a solid color that blends with the overall color scheme of the room. If you find a papier-mâché table that you particularly like at an antiques shop, work it into the room as a side table to an upholstered club chair with thick welting that emphasizes the outline of its shape.

In this sort of decorating scheme, a folding screen looks wonderful. It is practical, too, for creating a dressing area. Plain modern screens or simple wood panels that you have hinged together can be covered with wallpaper or paint. To further decorate a plain painted screen, add an old-fashioned feeling to the room by hanging a Victorian mirror on the outside.

Wall-to-wall carpeting in an exuberant floral pattern immediately sets a Victorian tone in a room that represents a mixture of styles. Or, you can choose a single solid color and on top of that lay a needlepoint design throw rug or Oriental carpet.

Blend styles as well as old and new fixtures for an eclectic lighting scheme. A ceiling fan with an attached light fixture also looks stunning in an eclectic room; contemporary lamps made of black rubber add to the visual drama. To soften this unabashedly modern element, place a Victorian lamp on the bedside table or an art deco torchere in a corner.

You may want to reverse this arrangement, however, and blend the Victorian fixtures with eighteenth-century Georgian wall sconces. While authentic pieces are extremely expensive, modern reproductions are plentiful—and reasonably priced—at retail. With their visual brilliance, they add a sense of glitter to the burnished brass and soft etched glass of the Victorian pieces and set an elegant tone in the room.

In this setting, you can indulge in accessories. Paisley and mohair throws on upholstered furniture soften the room, while collections of crystal, glass, and ceramics will make it sparkle.

MINIMAL

While the bed usually sets the tone of a bedroom, within a minimal setting it generally blends into the background to create the seamless look preferred by designers who work in this style. So, if you prefer the minimal look, select a platform bed with carpeted supports and use other furnishings to add the Victorian element.

An effective way to emphasize nineteenth-century furnishings is to treat them as sculpture. In a bedroom with an adjacent dressing room, interior designer Michael Braverman of New York City suggests placing a large secretary paired with a modern chair. This creates a quiet setting to pay bills, plan the week's activities, or simply sit and enjoy a good book. If the bedroom must also accommodate dressing and grooming, rather than use a

Flouncy bed dressings are at the heart of today's Victorian look. Here, designed by Burlington, they draw attention to a delicate iron bed in an attic room.

Waiting to be worn, this pearl necklace rests on a beautifully embellished bedroom dressing table that is framed by a wide border of antique embroidery.

A wall of old logs and rough sawn cedar is a rustic foil for a beautifully sculpted wicker chair. Dolls clothed in antique lace dresses add a playful Victorian touch.

secretary, choose a large armoire to store clothing and other gear.

A balloon-back or Renaissance chair placed next to a modern table on which you've placed an avant-garde lamp is a subtler way to add a Victorian flavor. For upholstery, select a moire or damask evocative of the past but in a minimalist color such as black. Or, go completely contemporary and upholster the chair in leather that is tufted in the nineteenth-century manner.

For the merest—but incredibly dramatic—hint of Victoriana, buy a damaged chest and hang the door on the wall as if it were a painting. When lit by an uplight sitting on the floor, the chest door creates an interesting interplay of light and shadow that makes it the focal point of the room.

On the wall by the bed, add a granite ledge one or two feet above the floor to hold such modern conveniences as a clock radio, stereo equipment, or television set. The ledge can be left plain, decorated simply with a long lace runner much like the kind that were used on the center of nineteenth-century dining tables, or serve as a nightstand to hold a Victorian brass lamp with an etched glass shade.

ROMANTIC

Nothing imbues a romantically designed bedroom with a Victorian feeling like a canopy bed. Draped with frilly lace trimmed with scalloped ruffling, the bed takes center stage particularly when the lace is repeated on pristine white coverlets and throw pillows. At the foot of the bed, add a small bench with an exposed wood frame that is upholstered in a light-toned chintz. Repeat this upholstery on an occasional chair

In this romantic bedroom a white iron-stone pitcher-and-bowl set becomes a vase for a beautiful bouquet of lilacs. The flowers repeat the colors of the floral-patterned fabric on the walls and the matching upholstered headboard.

Softly romantic, this bedroom dressing table is framed by tightly gathered drap-eries and a table skirt in a Victorian-inspired rose pattern on a sea green back-ground. In front of a clutter of bottles and accessories, the owner has placed a white wicker chair with a thick seat cushion and a ruffled pillow.

set near the dressing table. You can also use the chintz to section off a space with a mirror and vanity.

Beside the bed, place a wicker table that is large enough to hold a standing lamp with a ruffled lampshade and a small bouquet of colorful flowers, or, choose a metal table decorated with "filigree" of cast iron.

The bed and table can be supplemented with other furnishings. A rectangular dressing table from the late Victorian Age can be embellished with a fabric skirt, then decorated with a mirror on a stand, white ceramic pots filled with flowering plants, and silver-backed brushes. Photographs in old nineteenth-century frames make a beautiful display on the table, as do old jewelry, dolls, or clocks sumptuously placed on fine fabrics.

On the windows incorporate a one-foot deep valance and side draperies in a matching pattern that hang to the floor. Behind these, light lace sheers can be added as undercurtains to filter the light during the day. For an extra touch of detailing, place pots brimming with flowers on the windowsill if it's deep enough. Decorative plates mounted on the wall or a hook rack displaying vintage clothing are other accessories that will look smashing in this setting. A small shelf loaded with small-scale ceramic figures of animals and cut crystal objects also looks nice.

COUNTRY

Set the tone in this setting with an old iron bed that has delicate lines and fluffy bedcovers. At the foot of the bed, place a bench or old footstool draped with a paisley or mohair throw that is purely for display.

Bibelots *en masse* are called for here. Japanese ceramics and other Oriental figurines are attractive, but for a more rural feeling, substitute old ceramic crocks and carved-wood accessories with a primitive look. Old clothes can be hung on the wall.

Country decorating is much more formal in England than America, as this example clearly shows. Here, a skirted chair and tea table create a reading corner amid a plethora of accessories.

An old dresser visually anchors a bedroom that reflects the essence of the American-country decorating style. The plank floor and primitive rug reinforce the feeling.

The interplay of wainscoting, a needlepoint rug, and striped wallpaper evoke the Victorian spirit in the bedroom of an old, completely renovated home.

To display a range of textile products all at once, the stylist who composed this advertising photograph borrowed a nineteenth-century decorating theme—excess. Every imaginable bed dressing has been ladled on indiscriminately here. Could anything else fit? Certainly not a person wanting sleep.

Jeffrey Weiss

Robert Perron

In a rustic cabin, this shiny brass bed adds sparkle to the extensive woodwork and imbues the simple country-style space with a Victorian sensibility.

For other accessories, arrange a collection of old clocks or eyeglasses to immediately create the cozy atmosphere essential to the country look. A large table set to the side of the bed can be piled with nineteenth-century novels and can hold a brass lamp with a fluted glass shade. Be creative as you search through country flea markets and auctions.

Stenciling is right at home in the country-style bedroom. Borders can be painted directly on the floor as well as around the ceiling. For inspiration, look to old wallpaper border patterns or modern reproductions. William Morris papers are a good starting point here. Many local libraries have books that illustrate these patterns in their fine arts section.

For a color scheme, borrow from the country palette and choose rich tones like light red, husk, sienna, and harvest gold. For a true touch of country, however, simply whitewash the walls and accent woodwork such as ceiling beams with a dark stain. Personal memorabilia fit perfectly on the dressing table. Scour the antiques shops for crystal bottles, particularly those with silver caps, and add a lot of photographs, ivory combs, and old brushes from traveling kits.

Phillip Ennis

CHAPTER SEVEN

THE SPECIAL PLACE

◆　　◆　　◆　　◆　　◆

In some modern houses the library remains a room for reading and reflection much as it did during the Victorian Age. Yet in other contemporary homes, it has become a room for relaxation and play as either a family room, den, or media space. In a growing number of homes, the library has become an at-home office for entrepreneurs and professionals. Regardless of how you utilize special places such as these, they can reflect a distinctive appreciation of the Victorians' decorative arts.

HOME OFFICES

In designing a work space, you will want to consider your needs carefully. You will need a work surface, storage areas, and perhaps, seating for clients or customers. The easiest way to evoke the Victorian era in an at-home office—and give yourself plenty of work room at the same time—is to select an oak rolltop desk. Fitted with drawers on either side of the knee-hole and with pigeonhole spaces at the top, a rolltop desk supplies abundant storage space as well as a generously proportioned work surface for writing, reading, and tallying figures. If you have a tendency to leave your work spread out, a rolltop desk easily conceals the clutter. Most models include a top shelf where you can stack magazines, reference books, or frequently consulted papers close at hand. The shelf may also provide

An elaborate window treatment—scalloped undercurtains and brightly patterned draperies—become the focal point in this elegant study. Besides emphasizing the height of the room, the draperies create a colorful foil for the furnishings.

space for photographs and accessories that give the room a personal touch and help distinguish it from a business office in a high-rise building.

Genuine rolltop desks are plentiful at country auctions and antiques shops. The latter sometimes have "Derby" desks, which because of their quality construction, are among the most desirable of the rolltop models, at prices in the $2,500 to $3,000 range. For other mid-nineteenth-century models expect to pay about $1,750 at an antiques shop. Auctions in rural areas or small cities may have authentic rolltop desks that go for as little as $1,000.

Reproduction desks offer a satisfying alternative to the old originals. Holton Furniture of Thomasville, North Carolina, manufactures an oak desk with seven drawers, a locking rolltop, and seventeen pigeonholes. In keeping with the growing popularity of personal computers, Riverside Furniture of Fort Smith, Arkansas, has blended old and new together in the form of a rolltop

Courtesy of Motif

In a quiet study, lacy window curtains softly filter bright sunlight that illuminates an imposing round table and eclectic seating. The Victorian theme is carried through to the walls, which are covered with a paper patterned with colorful, exotic designs.

desk that doubles as a computer center. Designed to blend with traditional- and country-style decorating schemes, the desk provides hidden storage for a video display terminal, disk drive, keyboard, printer, and telephone jack. In addition, it contains electrical outlets and a built-in digital clock. Constructed of oak and pecan, the desk is sold at retail in department and furniture stores at a manufacturer's suggested price of $1,700.

An old swivel office chair on casters will supply comfortable seating at the desk, particularly when it is decorated with a soft loose cushion covered with needlepoint. For supplementary seating to confer with clients, consider an old mahogany armchair with an exposed wood frame upholstered in leather, or an occasional chair.

If your at-home office must also function as a guest room, this is an excellent opportunity to incorporate a convertible sofa into your design scheme. Though not in the least Victorian, a modern sleeper sofa with traditional camel-back styling and rolled arms will blend in with nineteenth-century furnishings and supply needed sitting and sleeping space. To further integrate this modern element into the room, add throw pillows covered with paisley or needlepoint. The sofa itself can be upholstered in any number of materials, including Victorian velvet, damask, or a pretty patterned chintz.

Today's business and professional ventures generate plenty of paperwork. So regardless of how much data your at-home computer stores, you will still need room to retain reference materials, old bank statements, documents, and the sundry files that successful professionals are required to maintain. Filing cabinets are probably the most efficient means, though they are not the most aesthetically pleasing. For this reason, you may want to utilize the abundant storage space that a large old Victorian armoire or bedroom wardrobe supplies. This type of piece is usually so large that it also can be used by weekend guests to store clothing and their personal effects.

If you must have the "hanging files" capacity, however, a file cabinet can be woven into a Victorian-inspired decorating scheme. One strategy is to conceal the cabinets in a closet. If that is not practical, don't despair. Instead of one tall, four-drawer cabinet, buy a pair of lower, two-drawer models and camouflage them. The most effective method is to have a round tabletop cut at the local lumberyard and place it atop the cabinets. Then drape the top to the floor with a sprightly patterned chintz fabric. Include whatever dressmaker details you prefer, such as rouching, ruffling, or piping. Flank each side of this "table" with a chair, and you have gained extra surface space for meetings or a light, midday lunch— without having to clean off your desk.

For additional storage, hunt the antiques and secondhand shops

Randy O'Rourke

Nineteenth-century patterns make this study come alive. They are used in true Victorian fashion on the wallpapered ceiling, draperies, and upholstery.

for an old nineteenth-century leather trunk embellished with brass nail heads. It makes a visually riveting coffee table and, placed in front of a sofa, hides old business records from view. Built-in banquettes instead of a sofa will also save space. During construction, ask your carpenter to place the seats on hinges so that you can lift them up and stack records directly on the floor. To blend a banquette into an otherwise Victorian room, upholster it in a gay chintz or another nineteenth-century-inspired fabric and add lots of throw pillows.

Lighting fixtures will vary depending on your overall design scheme. Rooms decorated in either the traditional, country, romantic, or eclectic manner easily accommodate table and wall-hung lamps with shades made of frosted glass, paper, or fabric including silk, damask, and moire. These types of fixtures also are appropriate in contemporary and minimal schemes, but here designers generally recommend a monochromatic shade that matches the color of the walls.

Your choice of accessories will be guided by the degree of formality in the room. A highly professional or impersonal office—even an office in an otherwise homey, residential setting—may not have any accessories. A more relaxed environment, on the other hand, may have many. Whatever you decide, accessories can vary from nineteenth-century portraits and landscape paintings to contemporary family photographs placed in old frames, candle-

An austere library gets a welcome sense of visual relief from a nineteenth-century table and Windsor chairs set atop an intricately patterned Oriental carpet.

sticks, ceramic figurines, and glass ornaments. An old oil lamp with a delicate glass globe is an especially nice piece to place on a shelf. Another touch that is both beautiful and practical is an old brass wall clock with Roman numerals.

MEDIA AND MUSIC ROOMS

The proliferation of sophisticated audio and video equipment geared specifically for residential use has spawned a new phenomenon—the media room. In many homes, an underutilized room is being transformed into an elaborate entertainment complex equipped to record and play back movies and television programs and mix audio tapes. Designing a media room, however, requires careful planning to insure adequate seating with unobstructed sightlines, sound control, and a sufficient power supply. In addition, the design must also provide storage space and facilities for serving food and drinks.

The heart of the media room is the electronic entertainment equipment. Generally, it is anchored by a large-screen television set flanked by tall storage units to house auxiliary equipment such as a videotape recorder, stereo equipment, and tape recorders. Old Victorian armoires are perfect for this sort of storage and imbue the room with a nostalgic air without interfering with its

Randy O'Rourke

Colorful wallpaper borders applied along the tops of the walls and at the corners give this room added architectural interest. A secretary conceals the television.

The elegance of the English countryside has been successfully transplanted to this American library. Awash with the bright hues of the sun, it represents a careful blending of several patterns of glazed chintz upholstery, balloon window shades, and a needlepoint rug. A careful attention to detail is reflected by the picture molding and a window seat from which to view a garden brimming with manicured plants.

In a traditionally inspired music room, the owners have successfully mixed several furniture styles including Windsor and round-back chairs.

The master of this house voices a strong preference for Victoriana in this unusual rendition of a media room. At the center of attention is an early phonograph, supplemented by a chaise longue and nineteenth-century window treatments with fringed tiebacks.

contemporary function. Also, because a large-screen television set is usually deeper than most standard cabinets, you can buy old damaged armoires and merely salvage the doors. Have a carpenter construct a new frame with modern internal brace supports.

If you prefer a conventional size television set, you can buy traditionally styled tall cabinetry, including armoires, at retail. Curtis Mathes of Dallas, Texas, manufactures a "Country American" armoire with oak doors and brass hardware. It is compatible in design with Victorian, traditional, and eclectic furnishings. Though it looks old on the exterior, the inside is thoroughly modern with adjustable shelves, a slide-out shelf, and a storage drawer. Another hidden pleasure offered by the same company is a "Traditional" wall system with a built-in twenty-five-inch television set and two curio cabinets flanking the central unit.

Low cabinetry that stores records and video and audio tapes while concealing speakers can bring the Victorian feeling into a room. With two cabinets flanking a large-screen television unit, you eliminate a jarring juxtaposition of old and new cabinetry, creating a seamless unity of form and function. You can find authentic Victorian chests at antiques shops and house sales, or you can buy a new low cabinet specifically designed to house electronic media equipment from Trend Line. The company's home-entertainment center—part of its "Cobble Square" collection—is made of oak and is designed to house a television set, stereo equipment, records, and bar accessories. Doors at the front of the unit open to provide access to the television set

and albums while the top tilts up to reach the stereo unit and bar.

For optimum viewing, seating around a large-screen television generally is in a horseshoe or U-shape. Though this calls for built-in banquettes and other custom pieces, there is no reason why the U-shape cannot be formed by a contemporary sofa and a Victorian ottoman and chaise longue arranged in a semicircle. With this approach, you can watch television programs as you recline on the chaise longue and the children play around the ottoman.

You also can add a Victorian flavor in the form of small bamboo tables on which your guests can place drink glasses and enjoy snacks while watching a movie. If your entertaining plans call for a bar, stock it with wonderful old Victorian glassware, decanters, and serving pieces recycled from the dining room. Then add cut crystal or silver accessories like candlesticks, decorative plates, and a large ceramic urn overflowing with colorful flowers. Visually soften these dramatic elements with a bountiful supply of needlepoint or other throw pillows embellished with fringe or ruffles.

Carpeting is almost a necessity in a media room to control sound. Usually designers specify wall-to-wall or fitted carpeting. If you choose either, ask your designer for one with a reproduction Victorian floral pattern. Or select a monochromatic, low-pile carpeting and place a needlepoint or Oriental rug on top of it.

The music room is closely allied in function with the media room. But, not only is the music room a place for listening to records and tapes, it can also be the scene of live performances for family members and friends. Indeed, the room is generally designed around the requirements of musical instruments for space, seating, storage, and acoustics.

Nothing sets a Victorian tone in a music room like a nineteenth-century grand piano that has been reconditioned and refinished. Because these antique musical instruments are expensive to buy and rehabilitate, you may prefer a modern piano. In that case, instead of a standard piano bench, select an old Victorian curved-back chair with an exposed wood frame and padded seat. Upholster the seat with needlepoint, chintz, or damask. A set of these chairs can be used to accommodate other musicians or guests. To elaborate on your Victorian theme, add old bentwood music stands rather than the modern chrome versions.

As in the media room, floorcoverings are important to control sound. In a music room, a fitted carpet that is covered with an Oriental or needlepoint rug will absorb sound, preventing it from bouncing off the walls and floor and creating a disturbing echo in the room. If you prefer the warm look of wood floors or the sleekness of bluestone, upholster the walls with a pretty chintz or more formal moire or damask fabric. Extra padding behind the

fabric will absorb even more sound. In addition, upholstered walls help contain the sound within the room so that activities in nearby spaces can continue without interference.

A nineteenth-century armoire makes a great storage space for sheet music, records, and musical instruments. You can conceal stereo equipment and bar equipment in them as well. For accessories, bring in Victorian ceramic candleholders and place them around the room or start a collection of Victorian vases and fill the room with the sweet fragrance of flowers all year long. This is also an excellent setting for potted plants in white wicker containers, ceramic pottery, and nineteenth-century art posters.

FAMILY ROOMS

Every family needs a private retreat away from the formality of the living and dining rooms. This is the essence of the family room or den—a casual space in which to watch television, play games, or simply enjoy each other's company. In planning a family room, interior designer Jean Harwood Davidson of Princeton, New Jersey, says she is frequently "tempted to do something a little more fun—like

An abundance of Victorian details gives this traditionally styled library a thoroughly nineteenth-century air. The atmospheric pieces—an Oriental carpet, wall sconces on either side of the fireplace, crisp glazed chintz upholstery, a Tiffany-style table lamp, and ornate picture frames.

Randy O'Rourke

Phillip Ennis

To create a study that doubles as a supplementary living area for small-group entertaining, the owners embraced Victorian decorative arts. Their choices range from a needlepoint rug with a floral pattern to splashy-patterned window draperies, botanical prints, and beautiful crown and baseboard moldings.

Randy O'Rourke

Interior designer Leah Lenney freely incorporated modern interpretations of Victorian furnishings in decorating this traditional study. While the floorcovering evokes the image of a needlepoint rug, it is actually modern wall-to-wall carpeting with a Victorian pattern. The furnishings are reproductions. The ''bookshelves'' add an unusual touch.

Randy O'Rourke

In a corner of the room shown above, the table is set so that the owners can enjoy tea beneath a copy of a Victorian painting.

Sam Sweezy

Reflecting Victorian decorating at its best, this graceful study is visually anchored by the classically inspired lines of the fireplace. A comfortable grouping of chairs rests on an Oriental rug, while overhead a nineteenth-century light fixture softly illuminates the room. Thick crown and baseboard molding frames the subtly patterned carpet.

papers in a grain pattern while Cowtan & Tout, also in New York City, offers several papers that look like sponge painting. Each of these is available in several colorways including green, blue, beige, and gray.

Exposed rafters add architectural interest in a family room and enhance the relaxed ambience. A wallpaper in a casual pattern that gives the effect of coffering on the ceiling is another alternative. Floor treatments can be equally informal with wool rag rugs from Heritage Rugs in Lahaska, Pennsylvania. These should reinforce the color scheme, which can be a soothing soft pink or blue with accents of green and cream.

A number of accessories are appropriate in decorating a family room or den. Papier-mâché serving trays are both decorative and practical while nineteenth-century watercolors and drawings will further your Victorian theme. At the end of a long, hard day, relax and prop up your feet on a Victorian footstool and gaze at a newly started collection of lovely old glass decanters or Victorian board games from James II Galleries Ltd. in New York City.

STUDIES AND LIBRARIES

This is the setting for quiet activities—reading, writing, and reflecting. Though you want to create an inviting environment, it should also be serene. There are few things that provide that emotional comfort like Victorian furnishings with their generous proportions and solid construction.

Placing a round or rectangular Victorian table in the center of a small library immediately evokes a classical feeling. Surround the table with side chairs and illuminate its surface with a hanging fixture such as a billiards lamp or small chandelier. With this arrangement, you can easily use the library as an auxiliary space for intimate dinners or to conduct a business meeting at home, secluded from other family activities.

For storage, line the walls with case goods—either nineteenth-century wardrobes or modern pieces depending on your particular design scheme. Even in a small space, these will be able to store numerous books and conceal small electronic appliances such as a portable television set or stereo system.

In a larger room, you may have sufficient space for a pair of upholstered Chesterfield chairs arranged in a sun-splashed corner as a separate sitting area for reading. To upholster the chair, choose a patterned chintz fabric from Lee Jofa, Inc., or Rose Cumming Inc., both in New York City. Brunschwig's "Harrow Damask," a cream floral pattern on a green and burgundy background, is another lovely printed cotton chintz with a Victorian sensibility.

rustic twig furniture." This is particularly fitting, as these pieces of furniture can be used in the winter in the family room, then taken outdoors onto the patio or deck in the summer. Another excellent suggestion is wicker, which can be painted mauve, green, or blue and fitted with a smocked seat and back cushions to create a more feminine atmosphere in the room.

If your family room doubles as a game room, move in a Ping-Pong table, chess set, or dart board. But, for a striking addition that fits perfectly into the Victorian atmosphere, buy an old billiards table. Blatt Billiards in New York City sells antique tables and will construct a new one based on your own design, whether it is nineteenth-century or contemporary.

For backgrounds, consider treating the walls with textured paint or a sponge-paint finish, or with wallpaper that simulates these treatments. Brunschwig & Fils in New York City sells

THE OUTDOOR SPACE

◆ ◆ ◆ ◆ ◆

The Victorians were avid gardeners. Their gardens were large in scale and filled with exotic plants and trees imported from around the world. The Victorians dotted their gardens with gazebos and garden seats where they took tea, ate luncheon, and conversed in private, traditions that continue today. Your preference may be for a gazebo, a modern greenhouse, a more modest outdoor deck, or simply a screened porch. In any case, any of these can reflect a Victorian spirit.

Metal furniture painted a pristine white or a garden seat ringing a big shady tree is the simplest way to enliven a backyard garden. Wrought iron chairs with cushions based on Victorian designs are manufactured by Lyon-Shaw of Salisbury, North Carolina. Because trees vary considerably in their circumference, you will have to build your own garden seat. Plans for a lovely, hexagon-shaped seat with a latticework backrest are sold by U-Bild Enterprises of Van Nuys, California. The plans can be adapted to fit any size tree. This same company sells plans for more than 700 woodworking projects, including outdoor trellises.

The Victorians tended to use rustic furnishings. Along this line, you can choose twig pieces or those in the Adirondack style. Distinctly American in feeling, Adirondack furnishings date back to the 1870's when the great camps were established in Upstate

Not all sunspaces are located at the back of a house. This airy room serves as the entryway and is simply furnished with casual wicker, a sisal rug, an adapted sewing machine treadle, and many healthy plants.

New York by the wealthiest and most powerful families in America. Though they were called camps, these enclaves were anything but modest. In fact, many of them were composed of sprawling complexes of buildings that included a large main cabin, guest cabins, boat houses, and separate sleeping quarters. Furnishings combined the fashionable and the rustic—from oak pieces by White Furniture and Heywood & Wakefield, to mission-style furniture, and crafts by American Indians and local artisans. Today, antique twig furniture is available from Margot Johnson Inc. and Kelter-Malce in New York City. Added Oomph! in High Point, North Carolina, American Country Store and Zona in New York City, and Mary Darrah in New Hope, Pennsylvania, sell both old and reproduction twig pieces. New furniture based on old designs and construction methods is sold by Amish Country Collection in New Castle, Pennsylvania, Backwoods Furnishings of Indian Lake, New York, Daniel Mack and Pot Covers of New York City, Lodgepole Furniture in Jackson, Wyoming, and Made in Mendocino of Hopland, California.

Wicker and rattan furniture are equally fitting in a gazebo. They have the added advantage of being portable and can easily be taken indoors for the winter and placed in other rooms such as a sunroom, bedroom, or breakfast area. Old wicker pieces are available from a number of sources, including antiques dealers, yard sales, and house sales. New pieces based on nineteenth-century designs can be bought from a number of outlets. House of Wicker and Casual in Statesville, North Carolina, sells the Typhoon rocking chair as well as designs by O'Asian, Henry Link, and other lines. Bielecky Brothers of Woodside, New York, is another excellent source for wicker tables and balloon-back chairs. Fran's Basket House of Succasunna, New Jersey, offers unusual underscaled wicker tables and chairs suitable for use in small gazebos. Typhoon International of San Francisco sells the "Wellington" chair, which is a reproduction of a nineteenth-century rocking chair design.

Be aware that wood, wicker, and rattan furnishings need protection from sunlight and solar heat. Even if they are placed in an attached greenhouse, they are subject to the same extremes as the exterior of your house. To prevent drying and cracking, apply a coat of varnish or, if you prefer, a natural finish. Otherwise, paint the furniture a tone that complements your overall color scheme.

For upholstery, many designers recommend sturdy canvas in light colors that are less prone to fading. Other fabrics also can be used, but it is better if they are laminated for protection from the sun. Several manufacturers, however, offer plasticized fabrics. The Laura Ashley line has one of the wider selections. Besides being suitable for outdoor upholstery, plasticized fabrics make excellent shower curtains.

Greenhouses are for more than plants. This one doubles as a dining area and is imbued with a Victorian spirit in its Gothic-styled framing on the windows and in the chairbacks.

An old stairway reflects the Victorians' aesthetic sensibility. Here, craftsmen molded iron into delicate lines and intriguing patterns that are as appealing to the eye today as they were a century ago.

To create a comfortable adult hideaway, the owners of this Victorian cottage screened their front porch and added lovely antique wicker furniture.

Graced with antique wicker furniture, a balcony in a two-story passive solar sunspace becomes a cozy sitting area in which to contemplate the stars at night.

The sitting area is suspended above the heat-collecting area, which is furnished with exotic wicker floor lamps and unusual chairs painted a rich black. The chairs are arranged to look through an expanse of sliding glass doors and take in the view—a lush flower and herb garden.

Capped with a cupola, this rustic Victorian gazebo blends deftly with its country surroundings. This six-sided structure serves a multitude of functions as an outdoor dining space, as a children's playhouse, and as a peaceful setting for tea.

The curves of sculptural white wicker furniture serve as the perfect foil for the hard architectural lines of this soaring, two-story screened-in porch. Set on the diagonal to match the pattern of the flooring, the furnishings form a sundappled sitting area beneath a whirling paddle fan. Surrounding this peaceful setting is exquisite architectural detailing, including soaring ceiling beams and wall supports arranged in a modern interpretation of Oriental Victorian fretwork.

Purely contemporary lines of outdoor furniture are available from a number of sources. Ficks Reed, McGuire, and Brown Jordan are among the best known. Composed of lightweight metal frames and durable vinyl seat and back lacing, these pieces are practical for families that prefer not to bring outdoor furniture inside the house after each use. These pieces not only can be ordered to complement any color scheme but they also permit flexibility in that the frame and vinyl lacing can be ordered in different colors for an unusual, custom look.

GAZEBOS

Useful during the spring, summer, and early fall, a gazebo can be the scene of many family activities—weekend luncheons and dinners, a children's playhouse, or a setting in which to read the Sunday paper in solitude. Though custom gazebos can cost well over $5,000 to design and build, there are low-cost alternatives. Several companies sell precut, kit versions that can be built as a do-it-yourself project. Or you can buy the plans and have a carpenter construct the unit for you. Bow House of Bolton, Massachusetts sells the "Belvedeary" gazebo that resembles an ancient Chinese pagoda with the modern convenience of screened windows and a door for insect control. An open-air gazebo in the Victorian tradition with gingerbread trim is sold in kit form by The Gazebo and Porchworks of Puyall, Washington. Called the "Celebration" model, it is a six-foot hexagonal gazebo with seating capacity for three or four persons. The unit is embellished with turned posts, spindles, open "lace" scrollwork, a cedar shingle roof, and a wood floor and base. Gazebos in several styles and sizes are offered in kit form by California Lattice Company of Chico, California. Consisting of precut redwood and Douglas fir, these kits range in price from $695 to $1,595. A precut redwood kit in an octagonal shape is sold by Serendipity of Amarillo, Texas for $1,895 while Moultrie Manufacturing Company of Moultrie, Georgia, sells a premanufactured kit in cast aluminum for $2,000 including delivery. Papillon of Atlanta, Georgia makes a gazebo kit that combines wood with a metal roof, bench, and door for $2,350 including delivery charges.

Plans for gazebos are much less expensive. A.S.L. Associates of San Mateo, California, has plans for a hexagonal gazebo for $10. The finished product measures approximately eight feet on each side with a twelve-foot-high roof. U-Bild Enterprises of Van Nuys, California, offers plans for the Victorian Gazebo No. 603 for $2.50. This model measures eight feet square with an eleven-foot-high roof. Some thirty plans, including several Victorian models, are available from Sun Designs of Rextrom in Delafield, Wisconsin, from $11.95 to $22.95.

Because gazebos are exposed to the elements all year long, decorations should be portable so that they can easily be taken indoors and stored during the winter. Storage space can be built in under the seat, which usually rings the inside perimeter of the structure. Additional storage can be incorporated beneath some gazebos and concealed by decorative latticework that includes a door on hinges for easy access.

Window treatments are often called for in a gazebo for three reasons—to control the intensity of the sunlight admitted to the

Bridging two eras, this gazebo embodies the Victorians' love of lush gardens and classical, eighteenth-century design.

Simple yet elegant, a six-sided gazebo forms a perfect vantage point from which to enjoy the view of a dazzlingly bright garden. From the conical-shaped roof to the latticework surround, this structure is a straightforward interpretation of Victorian design at its best.

interior, to protect the occupants from sudden rainstorms, and to visually soften the stark lines of the wood structure. Tinted sheets of plastic fitted as shades that can be rolled up and out of sight into a recessed valance is one effective method. A blue, yellow, pink, or magenta shade casts a marvelous color on the interior of the gazebo and prevents sunburning on hot, clear days. If you prefer cloth window treatments, choose canvas, which can be fabricated as shades or draperies. Another option that creates a lovely billowing effect is gauze draperies. Though they are not as long-lasting or light shielding as plastic and canvas, they can be closed to protect adults and children from insects without sacrificing the view.

Lighting can be as simple as votive candles or hurricane lamps. For more flexibility that will heighten your enjoyment of a gazebo,

extend a power line from the main house and add electrified lanterns set on rheostats. Lamps can be any color, although pink will be more flattering to guests, while amber or yellow will help control insects. When you host a party, add large Japanese lanterns to reinforce a festive atmosphere.

Be easy on yourself, keeping accessories that must be transported indoors to a minimum. Perhaps all your gazebo will require is a simple table setting—cloth napkins, a lace tablecloth, stainless flatware, and plain china plates. Or you can accessorize with permanent architectural fixtures such as additional gingerbread from The Emporium in Houston, Texas. Other architectural elements fitting for a gazebo include a copy of a nineteenth-century weather vane atop the cupola or finials from Cumberland Wood Products in Pennsylvania.

Intricate detailing or wretched excess? No matter, because in this small-scale gazebo, the eccentric Gothic cupola and trim are in complete design harmony.

Spike Powell/EWA

A glass roof pours natural light into this serene, double-height greenhouse. A wrought-iron based dining table, wicker seating area, patterned-ceramic tile floor, and a profusion of leafy green plants beckon the owners to spend a lazy afternoon with a pot of tea, a friend, and the Sunday papers.

GREENHOUSES

One hundred years ago, the greenhouse was most often a separate glass structure reserved for the nurturing of plants and flowers that gave Victorian houses a springlike look throughout the year. Today, however, separate greenhouses are used almost exclusively by commercial nurseries. In a residential setting, the greenhouse has actually been brought directly into the living space. Here, it serves many functions—as a sunny breakfast room or auxiliary dining space, a den, guest room, or children's playroom. More and more, however, the greenhouse is being fitted with exercise equipment and hot tubs and utilized as an at-home spa.

At the same time, the greenhouse is proving practical as a way to collect the free heat of the sun to warm the house and reduce fuel bills. On bright winter days, sunlight streams through the glazing, allowing solar heat to warm the house via direct-gain. The amount of heat admitted into the rest of the interior is controlled by opening and closing the doors, which are usually the sliding-glass patio variety. Excess heat is absorbed by a thick, thermal mass floor consisting of crushed rock or concrete that is covered with a decorative layer of tile.

When the outdoor temperatures begin to fall at night, the floor reradiates the stored heat to maintain comfort. Deep roof overhangs shade the greenhouse from solar heat gain in summer. Many units are equipped with vents that exhaust unwanted warm air outdoors, enabling the sunspace to be taken advantage of throughout the year.

A typical premanufactured greenhouse measuring eight feet by twelve feet will cost about $4,000. To that you must add the cost of installation or preparation of the foundation. A number of companies manufacture greenhouses. Among the better known are Four Seasons Greenhouses of Farmingdale, New York, Sun System Solar Greenhouses of Commack, New York, Janco Greenhouses & Glass Structures of Laurel, Maryland, Lord & Burnham of Melville, New York, and Aluminum Greenhouses of Cleveland, Ohio.

You have more options in furnishing a greenhouse than a gazebo. Besides outdoor seating and dining tables, you can add more delicate bentwood furniture as well as contemporary sleeper sofas to accommodate weekend guests. Modern designs in wicker and rattan are also available. Ficks Reed offers the "Ambiance" collection that includes wicker armchairs and a center pedestal table with a glass top. The same company makes the "A la Carte" collection consisting of a love seat, chaise longue, and end table. The Trading Company of Vero Beach, Florida, manufactures the "Tuxedo" modular seating system of

Mike Nicholson/EWA

Inspired by the nineteenth-century design, this greenhouse incorporates rattan chairs with curved Renaissance backs and a round table draped to the floor with colorful fabrics. For a touch of eclecticism, the floor is paved with practical and beautiful Mexican ceramic tile.

Derek Fell

Recalling the great greenhouses of the nineteenth century, a miniature crystal palace seems right at home in a manicured garden where it nurtures fragile flowers for colorful bouquets all year long.

Robert Perron

In a contemporary greenhouse addition to a period Victorian house, the owners have placed simple rattan furnishings that do not compete with the imposing curve of the sunspace entryway. This placement has the added advantage of leaving the greenhouse thermal-mass floor free of furniture so that it can collect the maximum amount of solar heat during the day. Large potted ferns that were favored by the Victorians reinforce the hint of a nineteenth-century atmosphere and add a touch of humidity for comfort.

cane that includes a visually striking daybed. O'Asian of Compton, California, offers a six-foot-long wicker sofa with a single seat cushion and three plump pillows. Another chaise longue is sold by Willow & Reed of East Elmhurst, New York. Two companies known for their contemporary outdoor furniture designs, McGuire of San Francisco and Brown Jordan of El Monte, California also make rattan pieces. The "Regency" chair from McGuire can be ordered in one of thirty-six hand-applied finishes. Brown Jordan has the "Treillage" collection that includes a queen-size sleeper sofa and lamp table.

As a floorcovering in a solar greenhouse, most homeowners select ceramic tile, which can be applied directly atop the thermal mass floor. To add a Victorian flavor, have your tile setter design a Greek key pattern with a border. For a slightly more unusual

design, copy the pattern from the bottom of an old nineteenth-century wading pool. If your plans for the greenhouse do not include solar applications, a sealed wood floor can be installed and embellished with area rugs.

Crucial to any greenhouse is proper window treatment. Because these units are subjected to immense amounts of direct sunlight, the homeowner needs an effective means of controlling the amount of light allowed into the space. At night, of course, window coverings are necessary to preserve privacy. Austrian shades in a durable heavy-weave cotton or canvas set an old-world tone, as do insulated window quilts. These can be purchased, or you can make your own and cover them with a sprightly chintz or elegant damask. For a contemporary effect, install narrow slat blinds.

APPENDIX ONE

HOW TO WORK WITH A DESIGNER

◆ ◆ ◆ ◆ ◆ ◆

A professional interior designer brings a wealth of experience and skill to your project. He can and should do much more than give your home a Victorian air. A good designer will devise a plan that creatively and deftly meets your family's unique needs.

When you purchase the services of a designer, you are acquiring a professional's sensitivity to form and scale, eye for complementary color and texture, and knowledge of authentic and reproduction Victorian furnishings and materials. In addition, a good designer is well versed in the intricacies of space-planning and traffic patterns, and an expert at disguising all the practical thought and effort that goes into making a room beautiful. And all of this is based on a thorough grounding in the mechanics of lighting, ventilation, textiles, acoustics, hardware, cabinetry, and surface finishes.

Choose a designer with care. Begin by requesting a list of names from your regional chapter of one of the following professional organizations. In the United States, they are the American Society of Interior Designers (ASID), the American Institute of Building Design (AIBD), and for specialized projects, the National Kitchen and Bath Association (NKBA). In Canada, contact the Interior Designers of Canada for more specific information. And in the United Kingdom, the Society of Industrial Architects and Designers (SIAD), the British Institute of Interior Design, and the Interior Decorators' and Designers' Association are good sources.

Visit designer showcase houses and contact larger department stores that have their own design studios. Search through design and decorating magazines for work that appeals to you, and page through state, regional, and city magazines for detailed articles. Metropolitan newspapers usually feature the work of local designers in weekly design/home furnishings sections. Clip and label the photographs of work you like and keep them on file. This will help you generate a list of possible designers, and it will serve as a visual catalog of your sense of style.

As you contact designers and interview them, insist on seeing photographs of their work and ask for the names of former clients as references. If you can, arrange to visit these homes; the owners will provide you with information on the designer's reliability in meeting budgets and deadlines, and their homes will give you a three-dimensional view of the professional's work. Recommendations from friends are invaluable for the same reason. Examine the houses for practical and aesthetic problems. A beautiful room with uncomfortable furniture, awkward traffic patterns, a profusion of electrical cords, or bad lighting is a frustrating waste of time and money. Check, too, to see how well the designer's work holds up over time. Furniture that shows premature wear because of poorly chosen upholstery, scratched work surfaces that were once lovely but are too delicate, or windows that are draped with sun-ravaged fabrics are all problems to be noticed and avoided.

With the information you've collected, you'll be more comfortable in selecting your designer. Once you've made your choice, expect to pay a retainer fee, which will usually be deducted from the total cost of the project upon completion.

A good designer will want to delve into your personal preferences; he'll want to know your likes and dislikes in colors, materials, and accessories. He'll want to know how casual or formal your lifestyle is, what your entertaining requirements are, what activities each room must accommodate, how much storage you'll need, and what your budget is. You may have pets or love giving large parties or require extra storage space for your hoarded belongings. If you prefer spending most of your time in the kitchen or tend to do all of your reading in the bedroom, now is the time to speak up.

When these essentials have been established, the designer will prepare a proposal. This usually includes drawn-to-scale floor plans that indicate furniture groupings, built-in storage units, appliances, and other architectural features. The specifications will also include color selections, photographs of furnishings, and sample swatches for upholstery, draperies, and wall coverings. Some designers provide color renderings, or sketches, of how the finished rooms will look, and some are willing to act as consultants in the purchase of vases, art, sculpture, and small details such as suitable placemats, cutlery, and even napkins.

While the design proposal becomes the aesthetic framework for your relationship with the designer, a contract forms the legal basis. A typical draft outlines the design services you are purchasing and the fee, including labor, transportation, and materials. A small design project generally costs less than $25,000,

while a medium-sized job might run from $25,000 to $100,000.

Business practices vary. Some designers charge a flat fee that takes into account devising the plan, the extent of the work to be done, the materials that it will require, and the time the project will take to complete. Others levy a charge of twenty to twenty-five percent of the total job estimate. In a third method, the designer purchases the furnishings and materials at wholesale prices, charges you retail, and pockets the difference. Another fee structure is based on an hourly rate, especially if the job is small. Less-experienced designers charge approximately $30 to $40 an hour, while well-known designers often have rates of more than $150 an hour.

Your responsibilities go beyond selecting a designer and signing a contract. First, you must decide on a firm budget and organize your design priorities; clearly tell your designer what your needs are. The designer then has the responsibility to devise a plan using your guidelines; and if the plan should change and costs escalate, you and the designer should have worked out a predetermined limit to the costs.

Second, you must be precise about what you want; photographs are invaluable for this. They enable the designer to see what design scheme and type of furnishings you prefer. By expressing what you want, you help the designer create a framework of reference so that he can go about the actual work more effectively.

Third, this is your project; make certain you understand it thoroughly. Study the design proposal, contract, fee schedule, and estimates carefully. Verify that the furnishings, fabrics, decorative treatments, and other details agree with what you and your designer chose. Assume nothing; ask all questions that occur to you, and get all agreements in writing.

These steps minimize misunderstandings that might require revising work in progress, which is the single biggest obstacle to completing an interior design project on time and within budget. At the same time, however, you must remain flexible and cooperative. The designer is an expediter of materials that may be delayed or shipped in the wrong color. He is a scheduler who must orchestrate the work of upholsterers, carpenters, electricians, and other tradespeople. Any of these specialists may be delayed in finishing work on time for a number of valid reasons through no fault of the designer. When this occurs, patience is not a virtue—it's an absolute necessity.

Be fair throughout the project by being generous in your appreciation and direct, sincere, and brief in your complaints. Never lose sight of the fact that you, the designer, and the tradespeople are all working to make your home beautiful, comfortable, and unique—all that you want it to be.

Courtesy of Laura Ashley

What better way to spend a lazy afternoon than curled up on an overstuffed chaise longue with a good book? A bevy of ruffled pillows in a geometric design are combined deftly with a crocheted doily and a paisley patterned throw. The design of the intricate wall hanging creates the illusion of a carved chair back that blends imperceptibly with the rolled arm of the seating decorated with carved vines, leaves, and other naturalistic Victorian motifs.

APPENDIX TWO
SOURCES OF SUPPLY

Companies are listed alphabetically by last name (e.g. LAURA ASHLEY is found under "A").

CANADA

ANTIQUE FURNITURE

EARLY TIMES FURNITURE
4940 Kingsway
Vancouver, B.C.
(604) 438-8204

COLLECTOR'S SHOWCASE
723 Osborne St.
Winnipeg, Man.
(204) 452-9505

FORT ANTIQUES
823 Fort St.
Victoria, B.C.
(604) 383-5441

THE LION MASK ANTIQUES
624–17th Ave. S.W.
Calgary, Alta.
(403) 228-6834

PACIFIC ANTIQUES LTD.
1916 Fort St.
Victoria, B.C.
(604) 388-5311

ROYAL CITY ANTIQUES LTD.
22653 Dewdney Trunk Rd.
Maple Ridge, B.C.
(604) 463-4955

275 E. Eighth
Vancouver, B.C.
(604) 873-4267

BATHROOM FIXTURES & ACCESSORIES

ATTICA HISTORIC HOME
SUPPLIES LTD.
508 Discovery
Victoria, B.C.
(604) 382-4214

CREME DE LA CREME
ANTIQUES & INTERIORS
342 Queen St. East
Toronto, Ont.
(426) 366-3933

BEDS

THE BRASS BED
119 Yorkville Ave.
Toronto, Ont.
(416) 968-6932

DECORATIVE ACCESSORIES

AVENDALE ANTIQUES
1626 Bayview Ave.
Toronto, Ont.
(416) 487-4279

FABRICS & WALLCOVERINGS

LAURA ASHLEY
2110 Crescent St.
Montreal, Que.
(514) 284-9225

Place Ste. Foy
2452 Wilfred Laurier
Ste. Foy, Que.
(418) 659-6660

18 Hazelton Ave.
Toronto, Ont.
(416) 922-7761

1171 Robson St.
Vancouver, B.C.
(604) 688-8729

2901 Bayview Ave.
Willowdale, Ont.
(416) 223-9507

GLASS

ALPHA OMEGA STAINED
GLASS GALLERY & SUPPLIES
10593–101 St.
Edmonton, Alta.
(403) 424-4032

THE DOOR STORE LTD.
118 Sherbourne
Toronto, Ont.
(416) 863-1590

EUROPEAN ART GLASS LTD.
372 Slater
Winnipeg, Man.
(204) 586-7545

MEDIEVAL GLASS
104–5560 Minoru Blvd.
Vancouver, B.C.
(604) 178-4965

WATER GLASS STUDIO LTD.
1040 North Park
Victoria, B.C.
(604) 384-1515

HARDWARE

ANTIQUE DOOR &
HARDWARE
1750 Avenue Rd.
Toronto, Ont.
(416) 789-4074

LEE VALLEY TOOLS
2680 Queensview Dr.
Ottawa, Ont.
(613) 596-0350

OLD ENGLISH BRASS LTD.
6760–99th St.
Edmonton, Alta.
(403) 432-0385

REGENCY DECORATIVE
HARDWARE
5525 W. Boulevard
Vancouver, B.C.
(604) 263-1945

STAIRCASES

STEPTOE & WIFE ANTIQUES
3632 Victorian Park Ave.
Willowdale, Ont.
(416) 497-2989

UNITED KINGDOM

ANTIQUE FURNITURE

PETER ALLEN ANTIQUES
17A Nunhead Green
Peckham, London SE15

WILLIAM BEDFORD
ANTIQUES
76 Bedford Rd.
London N1

BENNISON'S
91 Pimlico Rd.
London SW1

R. BONNET
582 King's Rd.
London SW6

F.E. & A. BRIGGS LTD.
73 Ledbury Rd.
London W11

CANNONBURY ANTIQUES
LTD.
174 Westbourne Grove
London W11

GREAT BRAMPTON HOUSE
ANTIQUES
Madley,
Hereford HR2 9NA

OLD PINE
571–573 King's Rd.
London SW6

ARCHITECTURAL ELEMENTS & ORNAMENTS

ALBION DESIGN
12 Flitcroft St.
London WC2

ARISTOCAST LTD.
Bold St.
Sheffield, Yorkshire S9 2LR

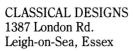

CLASSICAL DESIGNS
1387 London Rd.
Leigh-on-Sea, Essex

COPLEY CRAFTS
Thorney Grange, Spennithorne
Leyburn, North Yorkshire DL8
5PW

CHARLES HAMMOND LTD.
76 Harriett Walk
London SW1 9JQ

LONDON ARCHITECTURAL
SALVAGE SUPPLY CO.
Mark St.
London EC2

W.H. NEWSON
6 Pimlico Rd.
London SW1

ROGER PEARSON
Wentworth St.
Birdwell, Nr. Barnsley, Yorkshire

THOMAS & WILSON LTD.
454 Fulham Rd.
London SW6 1BY

WALCOT RECLAMATION LTD.
Walcot St.
Bath, Avon

BATHROOM FIXTURES & ACCESSORIES

ALBION HARDWARE LTD.
Simon House, Sunderland Rd.
Sandy, Bedfordshire SG19 1QY

ANDERSON CERAMICS LTD.
Dukesway, Team Valley,
Gateshead, Tyne & Wear NE11
0SW

BATH & BED SHOP
2 Russell St.
London WC2

CZECH & SPEAKE
39 Jermyn St.
London SW1

DANICO BRASS LTD.
31 Winchester Rd.
Swiss Cottage, London NW3

HILL HOUSE INTERIORS
Rotunda Bldgs.,
Montpellier Circus
Cheltenham, Gloucestershire

SANITAN
30–31 Lyme St.
London NW1

SITTING PRETTY LTD.
131 Dawes Rd.
London SW6

VIRGINIA
98 Portland Rd.
London W11

BEDS (METAL & BRASS)

AND SO TO BED
638–640 King's Rd.
London SW6

ANTIQUE BRASS BEDSTEAD
CO. LTD.
Baddow Antique Ctr.
Church St.
Great Baddow, Chelmsford,
Essex

THE BED CHAMBER
8 Symond St.
London SW3

MICHAEL J. COX
Lower Washbourne Barton
Ashprington, Totnes, Devon

DEPTICH LTD.
284–288 Western Rd.
London SW19

DREAMS
34 Chalk Farm Rd.
London NW1

GENERAL WOLFE ANTIQUES
General Wolfe Inn
Laxfield, Suffolk

CARPETING & RUGS

AXMINSTER CARPETS LTD.
Axminster, Devon EX13 5PQ

HARRODS
Knightsbridge, London SW1

LIBERTY & CO.
Regent St.
London W1

HUGH MACKAY & CO. LTD.
Roman House, Wood St.
London EC2Y 5BY

P & O CARPETS LTD.
5A Aldford St.
London W17 5PS

THOMSON SHEPHERD
CARPETS LTD.
112 High Holborn
London WC1

TEMPLETON CARPETS
525 Crown St.
Glasgow G5 9XR

CHRISTMAS DECORATIONS

COVENT GARDEN GENERAL
STORE
111 Long Acre
London WC2

HARRODS
Knightsbridge, London SW1

JOHN LEWIS DEPARTMENT
STORE
Oxford St.
London W1

PAPERCHASE
213 Tottenham Court Rd.
London W1

DECORATIVE ACCESSORIES

ANTICHITA
23 Molyneux St.
London W1

ANTIQUARIUS
135 King's Rd.
London SW3

556 ANTIQUES
556 King's Rd.
London SW6

S.A. COOK & SON
279 Finchley Rd.
London NW3

ZAL DAVA
26A Munster Rd.
London SW6

JUDY GREENWOOD
657 Fulham Rd.
London SW6

LANGFORDS
Oldebourne House,
46–47 Chancery Ln.
London WC2

LUCKY PARROT (ANTIQUES &
THINGS)
2 Bellevue Parade,
Bellevue Rd.
Wandsworth Common,
London SW17

MASSADA ANTIQUES
45 New Bond St.
London W1

OLD PINE
571–573 King's Rd.
London SW6

FABRICS

LAURA ASHLEY
Carno, Powys, Wales

G.P. & J. BAKER LTD.
17 Berners St.
London W1

C.V. HOME FURNISHINGS
LTD. (DORMS)
Newtown Mill,
Lees St.
Manchester M27 2DD

DESIGNERS GUILD
271 & 277 King's Rd.
London SW3

THE FABRIC SHOP
6 Cale St.
London SW3

LIBERTY & CO. LTD.
Regent St.
London W1

OSBORNE & LITTLE
304 King's Rd.
London SW3

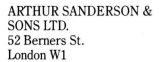

ARTHUR SANDERSON &
SONS LTD.
52 Berners St.
London W1

SEKERS FABRICS LTD.
15–19 Cavendish Pl.
London W1

WARNER'S FABRICS
7–11 Noel St.
London W1

FIREPLACES & ACCESSORIES

ACQUISITIONS
269 Camden High St.
London NW1

AMAZING GRATES
61 High Rd.
East Finchley, London N2

IDEAL FIREPLACES
300 Upper Richmond Rd. West
London SW14

ROGER PEARSON
Wentworth St.
Birdwell,
nr. Barnsley, Yorkshire

MR. WARDLE'S WORKSHOP
200–202 Garratt Ln.
London SW18

DOORS & HARDWARE

A & H BRASS LTD.
Dept H.M.G.,
201–203 Edgware Rd.
London W2

J.D. BEARDMORE & CO. LTD.
3 Percy St.
London W1

CATCHES & LATCHES
23 Fortune Green Parade,
Finchley Rd.
London NW11

HOUSE OF BRASS
Dept. HG, 122
N. Sherwood St.
Nottingham, Notts

KNOBS & KNOCKERS LTD.
36–40 York Way
London N1

GARDEN ACCESSORIES

CLIFTON NURSERIES
Clifton Villas,
Warwick Ave.
London W9

CROWTHER'S
Syon Lodge
Syon, Middlesex

GARDEN CRAFTS
158 New King's Rd.
London SW6

HOUSE OF STEEL
400 Caledonian Rd.
London N1

POTSI PURVEY (HG)
St. Mary's House,
2 Lower Bar
Newport, Shropshire

WHICHFORD POTTERY
Whichford, nr. Shipston-on-Stour
Warwickshire

GAZEBOS & OUTDOOR STRUCTURES

AMDEGA LTD.
Dept. H9/84,
Faverdale, Darlington
County Durham DL3 OPW

ALEXANDER BARTHOLOMEW
CONSERVATORIES
83 Disraeli Rd.
London SW15

JOHN CROSSLEY HOLLAND
Oxford Gallery,
23 High St.
Oxford

T. CROWTHER & SON
282 North End Rd.
London SW6

CHRISTOPHER HARTNOLL
Little Bray House
Brayford, North Devon

MACHIN DESIGNS
4 Avenue Studios
Sydney Close, London SW3

MARSTON & LANGINGER
Hall Staithe
Fakenham, Norfolk

TREVETT & CO. LTD.
Nuffield Ind. Estate
21 Cowley Rd.
Poole, Dorset BH17 7UJ

GLASS

ARCHITECTURAL HERITAGE
Boddington Manor
Boddington, nr. Cheltenham,
Gloucestershire

BRITISH SOCIETY OF
MASTER GLASS PAINTERS:
THE SECRETARY
115 Woodward Rd.
London SE22 8UP

GRAPHIC GLASS STUDIOS
One Munster Mews,
323 Lillie Rd.
London SW6

PILKINGTON FLAT GLASS
LTD.
St. Helen's, Merseyside WA10
3TT

WHITEWAY & WALDRON LTD.
305 Munster Rd.
London SW6

KITCHEN FURNITURE

ASHWORTH'S COUNTRY
WORKSHOP
Smiths Ln.,
Snitterfield,
Stratford-upon-Avon,
Warwickshire

CHATTELS
53 Chalk Farm Rd.
London NW1

HILL HOUSE INTERIORS
Rotunda Bldgs.
Montpellier Circus
Cheltenham, Gloucestershire

THE ORIGINAL KITCHEN
COMPANY
146A Penwith Rd.
London SW18

LIGHTING, FIXTURES, & LAMP SHADES

AFTER DARK
192 Fulham Rd.
London SW10

FRANKLITE LTD.
One Bridgeturn Ave.
Old Wolverton Rd.
Wolverton, Milton Keynes MK12
5QL

LAMP WORKSHOP
613–615 King's Rd.
London SW6

MR. LIGHT
279 King's Rd.
London SW3

TURN ON LTD.
116-118 Islington High St.
Camden Passage, London N1

CHRISTOPHER WRAY
LIGHTING EMPORIUM
New King's Rd.
London SW6

MOULDINGS & MILLWORK

ARISTOCAST LTD.
Bold St.
Sheffield, Yorkshire S9 2LR

HODKIN & JONES LTD.
515 Queen's Rd.
Sheffield, Yorkshire S2 4DS

GEORGE JACKSON & SONS
LTD.
Rathbone Works,
Rainville Rd.
London W6

PERIOD MOULDINGS LTD.
11A Westgate St.
Gloucester, Gloucestershire

THOMAS & WILSON
454 Fulham Rd.
London SW6

NEEDLEPOINT KITS

GLORAFILIA
The Old Mill House,
The Ridgeway
Mill Hill Village,
London NW7 4EB

HARRODS
NEEDLEWORK DEPT.
Knightsbridge, London SW1

JOHN LEWIS DEPARTMENT
STORE
Oxford St.
London W1

LUXURY NEEDLEPOINT
36 Beauchamp Pl.
London SW3

THE NEEDLEWORK SHOP
68 Welbeck St.
London W1

WOMEN'S HOME INDUSTRIES
LTD. (TAPESTRY SHOP)
85 Pimlico Rd.
London SW1

PAINTED FINISHES

ARTEX PRODUCTS LTD.
Artex Ave.
Newhaven, East Sussex

CUPRINOL LTD.
Adderwell, Frome
Somerset BA11 1NL

INTERNATIONAL BUILDING
PAINTS
24–30 Canute Rd.
Southampton, Hampshire S09
3AS

RUSTINS LTD.
Drayton Works Waterloo Rd.
London NW2

STERLING RONCROFT
Chapeltown
Sheffield S30 4YP

PAINTS & COATINGS

BERGER PAINTS, COLOUR
SCHEME SERVICE
Berger House,
Berkeley Sq.
London W1

CROWN DECORATIVE
PRODUCTS LTD.
Crown House,
Hollins Rd.
Darwen, Lancashire BB3 OBG

ICI (PAINTS DIV.)
Wexham Rd.
Slough, Bucks SL2 5DS

JOHN S. OLIVER LTD.
33 Pembridge Rd.
London W11

ARTHUR SANDERSON &
SONS LTD.
52 Berners St.
London W1

PUBLICATIONS

ANTIQUE COLLECTING
Journal of the Antique Collector's
Club
5 Church St.
Woodbridge, Suffolk

*THE GARDENER'S
CATALOGUE*
Country Garden,
Binns Close
Coventry CV4 9UJ

GOOD HOUSEKEEPING
72 Broadwick St.
London W1V 2BP

HOMES AND GARDENS
King's Reach Tower,
Stamford St.
London SE1 9LS

HOUSE AND GARDEN
Vogue House,
Hanover St.
London W1R OAD

NATURALLY BRITISH
mail-order catalog
13 New Row
London WC2N 4LF

PLEASURES OF PAST TIMES
11 Cecil Ct.
London WC2

ANNUAL
Journal of the Victorian Society
One Priory Gardens
Bedford Park, London W4

REPRODUCTION FURNITURE

BRIGHTS
Kingston House,
High St.
Nettlebed, Oxfordshire

DUCAL LTD.
Moiety Rd.
London E14 8ND

POOLE CRAFT STUDIOS
Great Yeldham, Essex

THIS AND THAT
50 & 51 Chalk Farm Rd.
London NW1 8AN

TOWN & COUNTRY PINE
Station Rd.
Princes Risborough, Bucks HP17
9DN

THE VILLAGE WORKSHOP
162 Wandsworth Bridge Rd.
London SW6

YOUNGER FURNITURE
(LONDON) LTD.
Monier Rd.
London E3 2PD

STENCIL KITS

LYN LE GRICE
Wells Head,
Temple Guiting
Gloucestershire GL54 5RR

PAPERCHASE
213 Tottenham Court Rd.
London W1

CAROLYN WARRENDER
One Ellis St.
London SW1

TILES

THE ART TILE COMPANY
Brickiln Ln.,
Etruria
Stoke-on-Trent, Staffordshire

CERAMIC TILE DESIGNS
56 Dawes Rd.
London SW10

JACHFIELD WORKS
Jackfield,
Ironbridge, Shropshire

H. & R. JOHNSON
Highgate Tile Works,
Tunstall,
Stoke-on-Trent, Staffordshire

THE REJECT TILE SHOP
178 Wandsworth Bridge Rd.
Fulham SW6

RYE TILES
The Old Brewery
Wishward, Rye, Sussex

TOWNSENDS
One Church Street
London NW8

WINCHESTER TILE CO. LTD.
Moorside Rd.
Winnall,
Winchester, Hampshire

WORLD'S END TILES
British Rail Yd.
Silverthorne Rd.
London SW8

WALLCOVERINGS

COLE & SON (WALLPAPER)
LTD.
18 Mortimer St.
London W1

HILL & KNOWLES
133 Kew Rd.
Richmond, Surrey TW9 2PN

PAPER MOON
12–13 Kingswell,
58–62 Heath St.
London NW3 1EN

STOREY DECORATIVE
PRODUCTS
White Cross,
Lancaster, Lancashire LA1 4XH

WATTS & CO.
7 Tufton St.
London SW1

See also Laura Ashley, Designer's
Guild, Osborne & Little, and
Arthur Sanderson & Sons Ltd.
under "Fabrics."

WICKER, RATTAN, & BENT WILLOW FURNITURE

CANE & TABLE
36 Rosslyn Hill
London NW3

COLOURFLAIR
4 & 7 Westminster House
Kew Road
Richmond, Surrey

D.U.K. FURNITURE, VITREA
(MERCHANTS) LTD.
Boundary House,
91 Charterhouse St.
London EC1M 6HR

GRAHAM & GREEN
4 Elgin Crescent
London W11

HARRODS
CANE DEPT.
Knightsbridge, London SW1

ERIC KING ANTIQUES
203 New King's Rd.
London SW6

UNITED STATES

ANTIQUE FURNITURE

DIDIER AARON, INC.
32 E. 67th St.
New York, N.Y. 10021
(212) 988–5248

BOB BAHSSIN
Post Oak Gallery
2128 Boston Post Rd.
Larchmont, N.Y. 10538
(914) 834–7568

JEAN PAUL BEAUJARD
209 E. 76th St.
New York, N.Y. 10021
(212) 249–3790

JOAN BOGART ANTIQUES
Box 265
Rockville Center, N.Y. 11571
(516) 764–0529

MARGARET B. CALDWELL
142 E. 82nd St.
New York, N.Y. 10028
(212) 472–8639

E.J. CANTON
818 Morris Ave.
Lutherville, Md. 21093
(301) 252–1113

THE CHATELAINE SHOP
Box 436
Georgetown, Conn. 06829
(203) 226–5501

RICHARD AND EILEEN
DUBROW
Box 128
Bayside, N.Y. 11361
(212) 767–9758

MIMI FINDLAY ANTIQUES
1556 Third Ave.
New York, N.Y. 10028
(212) 534–6705

HAMILTON-HYRE
413 Bleecker St.
New York, N.Y. 10014
(212) 989–4509

PETER HILL INC.
Maplewood Manor
East Lempster, N.H. 03605
(603) 863–3656

MARGOT JOHNSON, INC.
40 W. 40th St.
New York, N.Y. 10018
(212) 703–5472

KATHY KURLAND
1435 Lexington Ave.
New York, N.Y. 10028
(212) 410–4421

H.M. LUTHER, INC.
61 E. 11th St.
New York, N.Y. 10003
(212) 505–1485

RICHARD McGEEHAN
Box 181
Bedford Hills, N.Y. 10507
(914) 241–3815

DON MAGNER
309 Henry St.
Brooklyn, N.Y. 11201

FLORIAN PAPP, INC.
962 Madison Ave.
New York, N.Y. 10021
(212) 288–6770

ARCHITECTURAL ELEMENTS & ORNAMENTATION

AA ABBINGDON AFFILIATES,
INC.
2149–51 Utica Ave.
Brooklyn, N.Y. 11234
(718) 258–8333

COUNTRY ACCENTS
Dept. CL
RD # 2
Box 293
Stockton, N.J. 08559
(201) 996–2885

CUMBERLAND WOODCRAFT
CO. INC.
805 S. Spring Garden St.
Carlisle, Pa., 17013
(717) 243–0063

THE EMPORIUM
2515 Morse St.
Houston, Tex. 77019
(713) 528–3808

MOULTRIE MANUFACTURING
CO.
Drawer 1179
Moultrie, Ga. 31776–1179
(800) 841–8674

PINECREST
2118 Blaisdell Ave.
Minneapolis, Minn. 55404
(612) 871–7071

URBAN ARCHAEOLOGY
137 Spring St.
New York, N.Y. 10012
(212) 431–6969

VINTAGE WOODWORKS
Dept. 362
Box 1157
Fredericksburg, Tex.
(512) 997–9513

WORLD OF MOULDING
3109 S. Main St.
Santa Ana, Calif. 92707
(714) 556–7772

BATHROOM FIXTURES & ACCESSORIES

AMERICAN STANDARD INC.
40 W. 40th St.
New York, N.Y. 10036
(212) 840–5100

AMES INDUSTRIES, INC.
1071 Avenue of the Americas
New York, N.Y. 10018
(212) 921–9666

BARCLAY PRODUCTS LTD.
424 N. Oakley Blvd.
Chicago, Ill. 60612
(312) 243–1444

BATH AND CLOSET
BOUTIQUE
139A Newbury St.
Boston, Mass. 02116
(617) 267–6564

EX-CELL HOME FASHION, INC.
261 Fifth Ave.
New York, N.Y. 10016
(212) 679-4597

KOHLER
Kohler, Wis. 53044
(414) 457-4441

THE RENOVATORS SUPPLY, INC.
3224 Northfield Rd.
Millers Falls, Mass. 01349
(413) 659-2211

THE SINK FACTORY
2140 San Pablo Ave.
Berkeley, Calif. 94702
(415) 540-8193

SHERLE WAGNER INTERNATIONAL INC.
60 E. 57th St.
New York, N.Y. 10022
(212) 758-3300

WICKERWARE INC.
2200 E. Venango St.
Philadelphia, Pa. 19134
(215) 831-8585

BED DRESSINGS & LINENS

ARTISAN'S COOPERATIVE
Box 216
Chadds Ford, Pa. 19317
(215) 388-1436

CAROL BROWN
Caravoca St.
Putney, Vt. 05346
(802) 387-5875

CAMBRIDGE TEXTILES
Cambridge, N.Y. 12816
(518) 677-2624

CARTER CANOPIES
Box 3372
Eden, N.C. 27288
(919) 623-6829

COUNTRY CURTAINS
Stockbridge, Mass. 01262
(413) 298-4938

CUDDLEDOWN
87 Pleasant St.
Yarmouth, Maine 04096
(207) 846-5759

GARNET HILL, INC.
Main St.
Franconia, N.H. 03580
(603) 823-5545

VIRGINIA GOODWIN
Box 36603
Charlotte, N.C. 28236
(704) 376-8786

PUCKIHUDDLE PRODUCTS
Oliverea, N.Y. 12462
(914) 254-5553

ROSEMONT
Laura Copenhaver Industries, Inc.
231 W. Lane
Marion, Va. 24354
(703) 783-4663

LUCY STEWART'S PRIVATE STOCK
Box 443
Grafton, N.H. 03240
(603) 523-4313

A TOUCH OF CLASS
Mechanic St.
North Conway, N.H. 03860
(603) 356-5769

WETHERSFIELD STATION
211 Maple St.
Wethersfield, Conn. 06109
(203) 529-1330

YUNGJOHANN HILLMAN CO.
1350 Manufacturing St.
Suite 221
Dallas, Tex. 75207
(214) 742-3496

BEDS

BEDLAM BRASS BEDS
19-21 Fair Lawn Ave.
Fair Lawn, N.J. 07410
(201) 796-7200

THE BEDPOST
Road 1
Box 155
Pen Argyl, Pa. 18072
(215) 588-3824

THE BRASS AND IRON BED CO.
Box 453
El Cerrito, Calif. 94530
(415) 526-5304

BRASS BED CO. OF AMERICA
2801 E. 11th St.
Los Angeles, Calif. 90023
(213) 269-9495

A BRASS BED SHOPPE
12421 Cedar Rd.
Cleveland Heights, Ohio 44106
(216) 371-0400

CANNONDALE'S HEIRLOOMS LIMITED
Cannondale Bldgs.
Rte. 113 South
Dept. 21801, Box 680
Berlin, Md. 21811
(301) 641-4477

DESIGN INNOVATIONS
8285 Jericho Tpke.
Woodbury, N.Y. 11797
(516) 367-8555

ISABEL BRASS FURNITURE, INC.
120 E. 32nd St.
New York, N.Y. 10016
(212) 689-3307

J/B ROSS
409 Joyce Kilmer Ave.
New Brunswick, N.J. 08901
(201) 246-0900

LISA VICTORIA BRASS BEDS
17106 S. Crater Rd.
Petersburg, Va. 23805
(804) 862-1491

ROBERTS BRASS CO.
24 Park Lane Rd.
New Milford, Conn. 06776
(203) 354-6142

CHARLES P. ROBERTS BRASS BED CO.
149 W. 24th St.
New York, N.Y. 10011
(212) 807-1989

BILLIARD TABLES

BLATT BILLIARDS
809 Broadway
New York, N.Y. 10003
(212) 674-8855

CABINETRY (MEDIA)

CURTIS MATHES
Box 223607
Dallas, Tex. 75222-0607
(214) 659-1122

TREND LINE FURNITURE CORP.
Div. of Mohasco Industries, Inc.
Box 188
Hickory, N.C. 28603
(704) 328-2521

CARPETS & RUGS

HERITAGE RUGS
Street Rd.
Lahaska, Pa. 18931
(215) 794-7229

LANGHORNE CARPETING CO.
Box 175
Penndel, Pa. 19047
(215) 757-5155

MOHAWK CARPET
919 Third Ave.
New York, N.Y. 10022
(212) 759-8320

MONSANTO TEXTILES CO.
1460 Broadway
New York, N.Y. 10036
(212) 382-9600

PATTERSON FLYNN & MARTIN
950 Third Ave.
New York, N.Y. 10022
(212) 751-6414

ROSECORE CARPET CO. INC.
979 Third Ave.
New York, N.Y. 10022
(212) 421–7272

SCALAMANDRE SILKS, INC.
950 Third Ave.
New York, N.Y. 10022
(212) 361–8500

SCHUMACHER
919 Third Ave.
New York, N.Y. 10022
(212) 644–5900

STARK CARPET CORP.
979 Third Ave.
New York, N.Y. 10022
(212) 752–9000

VICTORIAN COLLECTIBLES,
LTD.
845 E. Glenbrook Rd.
Milwaukee, Wis. 53217
(414) 352–6910

CHRISTMAS DECORATIONS

APEX INTERNATIONAL
200 W. Palmetto Park Rd.
Suite 102
Boca Raton, Fla. 33432
(305) 391–7038

JOAN COOK
3200 SE 14th Ave.
Ft. Lauderdale, Fla. 33160
(800) 327–3799

COUNTRY TOUCH
Rte. 2
Box 58
Columbus, Kans. 66725
(316) 389–2228

ERIC'S OF BOSTON
38 Charles St.
Boston, Mass. 02114
(617) 227–6567

FAITH MOUNTAIN
102 Main St.
Sperryville, Va. 22740
(800) 822–7238

HIGH COUNTRY
COLLECTIBLES
Rte. 3
Box 48
Jonesborough, Tenn. 37659
(615) 753–2726

PIECES OF OLDE
5614 Greenspring Ave.
Baltimore, Md. 21209
(301) 446–4949

B. SHACKMAN & CO., INC.
85 Fifth Ave.
New York, N.Y. 10003
(212) 989–5162

SIMPLE PLEASURES OF
TEXAS
720 Browning
Angleton, Tex. 77515

VISIONS OF SUGAR PLUMS
Box 355
Bosworth, Mo. 64623

WILDFLOWERS OF OREGON
The Old Church on Main St.
Halfway, Oreg. 97834
(503) 742–6474

CRAFTS

JOE A. TURNER
8600 Burton Way
Los Angeles, Calif. 90048
(213) 274–3020

DECORATIVE ACCESSORIES

MARVIN ALEXANDER INC.
315 E. 62nd St.
New York, N.Y. 10021
(212) 838–2320

THE AMERICAN HAND
19 Post Rd. West
Westport, Conn. 06880
(203) 226–8883

ANICHINI GALLERY
7 E. 20th St.
New York, N.Y. 10003
(212) 982–7274

CHERCHEZ
864 Lexington Ave.
New York, N.Y 10021
(212) 737–8215

THE COLLECTOR'S CABINET
153 E. 57th St.
New York, N.Y. 10022
(212) 355–2033

CUMBERLAND GENERAL
STORE
Rte. 3
Crossville, Tenn. 38555
(615) 484–8481

DECORATION DAY
2076 Boston Post Rd.
Larchmont, N.Y. 10538
(914) 834–9252

GORDON FOSTER ANTIQUES
1322 Third Ave.
New York, N.Y. 10021
(212) 744–4922

THE GAZEBO
660 Madison Ave.
New York, N.Y. 10021
(212) 832–7077

VITO GIALLO ANTIQUES
966 Madison Ave.
New York, N.Y. 10021
(212) 535–9885

HERITAGE CLOCK &
BRASSMITHS
Heritage Industrial Park
Drawer 1577
Lexington, N.C. 27293–1577
(704) 956–2113

HYDE PARK ANTIQUES LTD.
836 Broadway
New York, N.Y. 10003
(212) 477–0033

JAMES II GALLERY
15 E. 57th St.
New York, N.Y. 10022
(212) 355–7040

JERRYSTYLE
34 E. Fourth St.
New York, N.Y. 10003
(212) 987–5294

KAYNE & CO.
Sconset Sq.
Myrtle Ave.
Westport, Conn. 06880
(203) 227–0810

KENTSHIRE GALLERIES
37 E. 12th St.
New York, N.Y. 10003
(212) 673–6644

LIMITED EDITIONS
253 E. 72nd St.
New York, N.Y. 10021
(212) 249–5563

LONDON ANTIQUES
DEALERS
930 "E" St.
San Diego. Calif. 92101
(619) 238–9274

DIANE LOVE INC.
851 Madison Ave.
New York, N.Y. 10021
(212) 879–6997

J. GARVIN MECKING
ANTIQUES
72 E. 11th St.
New York, N.Y. 10003
(212) 677–4316

TREVOR POTTS
242 E. 72nd St.
New York, N.Y. 10021
(212) 288–0370

JOHN ROSSELLI ANTIQUES
255 E. 72nd St.
New York, N.Y. 10021
(212) 737–2252

SEDGWICK HOUSE
101 N. Tenth St.
Noblesville, Ind. 46060
(317) 773–7372

JOHNNY TREMAIN SHOP
Colonial Inn
Monument St.
Concord, Mass. 01742
(617) 369–1700

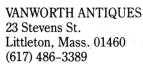

VANWORTH ANTIQUES
23 Stevens St.
Littleton, Mass. 01460
(617) 486-3389

VICTORIAN BOUQUET
53A Charles St.
Boston, Mass. 02114
(617) 367-6648

WOLFMAN, GOLD &
GOOD CO.
484 Broome St.
New York, N.Y. 10013
(212) 431-1888

THOS. K. WOODARD
835 Madison Ave.
New York, N.Y. 10021
(212) 988-2906

WOOLWORKS
838 Madison Ave.
New York, N.Y. 10021
(212) 861-8700

FABRICS & WALLCOVERINGS

LAURA ASHLEY
714 Madison Ave.
New York, N.Y. 10021
(212) 371-0606

BRADBURY & BRADBURY
WALLPAPERS
Box 155
Benicia, Calif. 94510
(707) 746-1900

BRUNSCHWIG & FILS, INC.
979 Third Ave.
New York, N.Y. 10022
(212) 838-7878

CLARENCE HOUSE
40 E. 57th St.
New York, N.Y. 10022
(212) 752-2890

COLLINS & AIKMAN CORP.
210 Madison Ave.
New York, N.Y. 10016
(212) 578-1200

COWTAN & TOUT, INC.
979 Third Ave.
New York, N.Y. 10022
(212) 753-4488

ROSE CUMMING, INC.
232 E. 59th St.
New York, N.Y. 10022
(212) 758-0844

GREEFF FABRICS, INC.
155 E. 56th St.
New York, N.Y. 10022
(212) 888-5050

HALLIE GREER, INC.
Cushing Corners Rd.
Box 165
Freedom, N.H. 03836
(603) 539-6007

GURIAN'S
276 Fifth Ave.
New York, N.Y. 10001
(212) 689-9696

HINSON & CO.
979 Third Ave.
New York, N.Y. 10022
(212) 475-4100

RALPH LAUREN HOME
FURNISHINGS
1185 Avenue of the Americas
New York, N.Y. 10020
(212) 930-3200

LEE JOFA INC.
979 Third Ave.
New York, N.Y. 10022
(212) 688-0444

KARL MANN ASSOCIATES
114 W. 17th St.
New York, N.Y. 10011
(212) 691-1585

MILLIKEN & CO.
1045 Avenue of the Americas
New York, N.Y. 10018
(212) 819-4200

OLD WORLD WEAVERS, INC.
136 E. 57th St.
New York, N.Y. 10022
(212) 355-7186

PIERRE DEUX
369 Bleecker St.
New York, N.Y. 10014
(212) 243-7740

RUE DE FRANCE
78 Thames St.
Newport, R.I. 02840
(401) 846-2084

SANDERSON FABRICS
979 Third Ave.
New York, N.Y. 10022
(212) 319-7220

SCALAMANDRE SILKS, INC.
950 Third Ave.
New York, N.Y. 10022
(212) 361-8500

SCHUMACHER
939 Third Ave.
New York, N.Y. 10022
(212) 644-5900

SHAMA IMPORTS
Box 2900
Farmington Hills, Mich. 48018
(313) 553-0261

THOMAS STRAHAN CO.
National Gypsum Decorative
Products
Corporate Pl. 128
Bldg. 3, Suite 25
Wakefield, Mass. 01880
(617) 246-5130

STROHEIM & ROMANN
155 E. 56th St.
New York, N.Y. 10022
(212) 691-0700

THE TWIGS
5700 Third St.
San Francisco, Calif. 94124
(415) 822-1626

IAN WALL
979 Third Ave.
New York, N.Y. 10022
(212) 758-5357

WAVERLY FABRICS
58 W. 40th St.
New York, N.Y. 10018
(212) 644-5900

GARDEN ACCESSORIES

ERKINS STUDIOS, INC.
406 Thames St.
Newport, R.I. 02840
(401) 849-2660

FLORENTINE CRAFTSMEN
46-24 28th St.
Long Island City, N.Y. 11101
(718) 532-3926

NEW YORK BOTANICAL SHOP
590 Madison Ave.
New York, N.Y. 10022
(212) 980-8544

GAZEBOS & OUTDOOR STRUCTURES

BOW HOUSE
Box 228
Bolton, Mass. 01740
(617) 779-6464

CUMBERLAND WOODCRAFT
CO., INC.
805 S. Spring Garden St.
Carlisle, Pa. 17013
(717) 243-0063

THE GAZEBO AND
PORCHWORKS
3901 N. Meridian
Puyall, Wash. 98371
(206) 848-0502

U-BILD PATTERNS FOR
LIVING
15241 Stagg St.
Box 2383
Van Nuys, Calif. 91409
(818) 785-6368

GLASS

THE BEVELED EDGE
865 Hillcrest Blvd.
Hoffman Estates, Ill. 60195
(312) 843-8960

THE BEVELING STUDIO
15507 NE 90th St.
Redmond, Wash. 90852
(206) 885-7274

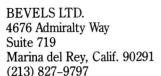

BEVELS LTD.
4676 Admiralty Way
Suite 719
Marina del Rey, Calif. 90291
(213) 827-9797

CENTER CITY STAINED
GLASS SUPPLY, INC.
926 Pine St.
Philadelphia, Pa. 19106
(215) 592-8804

PETER DAVID
8057 28th Ave. Northwest
Seattle, Wash. 98117
(206) 783-1731

SANDY MOORE
105 Wauwinet Trail
Guilford, Conn. 06437
(203) 457-1435

GREENHOUSES

FOUR SEASONS SOLAR
PRODUCTS CORP.
910 Rte. 110
Farmingdale, N.Y. 11735
(800) 645-9527

JANCO GREENHOUSES &
GLASS STRUCTURES
9390 Davis Ave.
Laurel, Md. 20707
(301) 498-5700

LORD & BURNHAM
2 Main St.
Irvington, N.Y. 10533
(914) 591-8800

NATIONAL GREENHOUSE CO.
Box 100
Pana, Ill. 62557
(217) 562-3919

SUN SYSTEM SOLAR
GREENHOUSES
60 Vanderbilt Motor Pkwy.
Commack, N.Y. 11725
(516) 543-7600

VEGETABLE FACTORY
71 Vanderbilt Ave.
New York, N.Y. 10169
(212) 867-0113

HARDWARE

ANTIQUE HARDWARE CO.
Box 1592
Torrance, Calif. 90505
(213) 378-5990

ARTISTIC BRASS
3136 E. 11th St.
Los Angeles, Calif. 90280
(213) 564-1100

CHICAGO FAUCETS
2100 S. Nuclear Dr.
Des Plaines, Ill. 60018
(312) 298-1140

CIRECAST INC.
380 Seventh St.
San Francisco, Calif. 94103
(415) 659-2211

CRAWFORD'S OLD HOUSE
STORE
301 McCall St.
Waukesha, Wis. 53186
(414) 542-0685

P.E. GUERIN
23 Jane St.
New York, N.Y. 10014
(212) 243-5270

HORTON BRASSES
Box 120
Cromwell, Conn. 06416
(203) 635-4400

KRAFT HARDWARE
300 E. 64th St.
New York, N.Y. 10021
(212) 838-2214

BRIAN F. LEO
7520 Stevens Ave. South
Richfield, Minn. 55423
(612) 861-1473

LITCHFIELD HOUSE
Church St.
Roxbury, Conn 06783
(203) 355-0375

PAUL ASSOCIATES
155 E. 55th St.
New York, N.Y. 10022
(212) 755-1313

RENOVATOR'S SUPPLY HOUSE
182 Northfield Rd.
Millers Falls, Mass. 01349
(413) 659-2211

ROY ELECTRIC
1054 Coney Island Ave.
Brooklyn, N.Y. 11230
(718) 339-6311

SUNRISE SPECIALTY
2210 San Pablo Ave.
Berkeley, Calif. 94702
(415) 845-4751

LAMP SHADES

BURDOCH SILK LAMPSHADE
CO.
Box 2633
Leucadia, Calif. 92024
(619) 458-1005

RUTH VITOW
160 E. 56th St.
New York, N.Y. 10022
(212) 355-6881

YESTERSHADES
3534 SE Hawthorne St.
Portland, Oreg. 97214
(503) 238-5755

MOLDINGS & MILLWORK

CLASSIC ARCHITECTURAL
SPECIALTIES
5302 Junius St.
Dallas, Tex. 75214
(214) 827-5111

DOVETAIL, INC.
Box 1569
Lowell, Mass. 01853
(617) 454-2944

FOCAL POINT
2005 Marietta Rd. Northwest
Atlanta, Ga. 30318
(404) 351-0820

NEEDLEPOINT KITS

ALICE MAYNARD
NEEDLEWORKS
133 E. 65th St.
New York, N.Y. 10021
(212) 535-6107

PAINTS & COATINGS

FULLER-O'BRIEN PAINTS
450 E. Grand Ave.
South San Francisco, Calif. 94808
(415) 761-2300

SHERWIN-WILLIAMS CO.
101 Prospect Ave. Northwest
Cleveland, Ohio 44115
(216) 566-2000

PUBLICATIONS

CENTURY OF COLOR
American Life Foundation
Box 349
Watkins Glen, N.Y. 14891

THE DESIGNER'S RESOURCE
5160 Melrose Ave.
Los Angeles, Calif. 90038
(213) 465-9235

THE OLD HOUSE JOURNAL
THE OLD HOUSE JOURNAL
BUYER'S GUIDE
69A Seventh Ave.
Brooklyn, N.Y. 11217
(718) 636-4514

VICTORIAN HOMES
MAGAZINE
Box 61
Millers Falls, Mass. 01349
(413) 659-3785

REPRODUCTION FURNITURE

AMERICAN FURNITURE
GALLERIES
Box 60
Montgomery, Ala. 36101
(800) 547-5240

FURNITURE TRADITIONS
Box 5067
Hickory, N.C. 28603
(704) 324-0611

HITCHCOCK CHAIR CO.
Box 507
New Hartford, Conn. 06057
(203) 379-8531

HOLTON FURNITURE CO.
805 Randolph St.
Thomasville, N.C. 27360
(919) 472-0400

MARTHA M. HOUSE
1022 S. Decatur St.
Montgomery, Ala. 36104
(205) 264-3558

KAYLYN, INC.
Box 2366
High Point, N.C. 27261
(919) 885-4125

MAGNOLIA HALL
726 Andover Dr.
Atlanta, Ga. 30327
(404) 237-9725

LEWIS MITTMAN INC.
214 E. 52nd St.
New York, N.Y. 10022
(212) 888-5580

RIVERSIDE FURNITURE CO.
Drawer 1427
Fort Smith, Ark. 72902
(501) 785-8100

VANGUARD FURNITURE CO.
Box 2187
Hickory, N.C. 28603
(704) 328-5631

STENCIL KITS

ADELE-BISHOP
Box 3349
Kinston, N.C. 28501
(800) 334-4186

TABLE LINENS

CAPRICE-GENI
KGM Industries
295 Fifth Ave.
Suite 1402
New York, N.Y. 10016
(212) 696-9500

GROSSMAN & WEISSMAN
295 Fifth Ave.
New York, N.Y. 10016
(212) 685-2026

JERHART INC.
2375 W. Armitage Ave.
Chicago, Ill. 60647
(312) 772-5000

LAYTON HOME FASHIONS
1420 NW Lovejoy
Portland, Ore. 97209
(503) 222-3847

QUAKER LACE
24 W. 40th St.
New York, N.Y. 10036
(212) 221-0480

TILE (DECORATIVE & FLOOR)

AMERICAN OLEAN TILE CO.
1000 Cannon Ave.
Lansdale, Pa. 19446
(215) 855-1111

LAURA ASHLEY
714 Madison Ave.
New York, N.Y. 10022
(212) 371-0606

COUNTRY FLOORS INC.
300 E. 61st St.
New York, N.Y. 10021
(212) 758-7414

WICKER, RATTAN, & BENT WILLOW FURNITURE

ADDED OOMPH!
270 W. Wrenn St.
High Point, N.C. 27262
(919) 886-4410

AMERICAN FOLK ART
354 Kennesaw Ave.
Marietta, Ga. 30060
(404) 344-5985

BACKWOODS FURNISHINGS
Rte. 28
Box 161
Indian Lake, N.Y. 12842
(518) 251-3327

BIELECKY BROTHERS
306 E. 61st St.
Woodside, N.Y. 11375
(718) 424-4764

ELLENBURG'S WICKER & CASUAL
Box 5628
Statesville, N.C. 28677
(704) 873-2900

KELTER-MALCE
361 Bleecker St.
New York, N.Y. 10014
(212) 969-6760

LODGEPOLE FURNITURE
Star Rte.
Box 15
Jackson, Wyo. 83001
(307) 733-3199

DANIEL MACK
225 W. 106th St.
New York, N.Y. 10025
(212) 666-4277

POTCOVERS
101 W. 28th St.
New York, N.Y. 10001
(212) 594-5075

JOHNNY TREMAIN SHOP
Colonial Inn
Monument St.
Concord, Mass. 01742
(617) 369-1700

VANWORTH ANTIQUES
23 Stevens St.
Littleton, Mass. 01460
(617) 486-3389

WALTERS WICKER WONDERLAND
991 Second Ave.
New York, N.Y. 10022
(212) 758-0472

WILLOW & REED
32-34 111th St.
East Elmhurst, N.Y. 11369
(718) 335-0807

THE WILLOW WORKS
267 Eighth St.
San Francisco, Calif. 94109
(415) 771-1938

ZONA
484 Broome St.
New York, N.Y. 10013
(212) 925-6750

WINDOW TREATMENTS

DESIGN PORTFOLIO
Box 5417
Takoma Park, Md. 20912

DOROTHY'S RUFFLED ORIGINALS, INC.
6721 Market St.
Wilmington, N.C. 28405
(800) 334-2593

A.L. ELLIS INC.
278 Court St.
N. Plymouth, Mass. 02360
(617) 746-1941

GREAT COVERUPS
Box 1368
West Hartford, Conn. 06107
(203) 521-2169

LOUIS HAND DIVISION
Aberdeen Mfg. Corp.
16 E. 34th St.
New York, N.Y. 10016
(212) 889-8380

KARPEL CURTAIN CORP.
261 Fifth Ave.
New York, N.Y. 10016
(212) 784-7160

INDEX

DESIGN CREDITS

Antine/Polo: 16
Bradbury and Bradbury: 76
Mario Buatta: 94 (left and right), 120
Centerbrook-Mark Simon/Alan Buchsbaum: 155
Eric A. Chase Architect: 36
Classic Galleries/Peg Heron and Claudia Dowling: 129
Gary Crain Interiors: 126
Dorothy Diamond: 21 (right), 66
Gus Dudley: 150
Isabelle Collin Dufresne: 118
Georgina Fairholme: 116, 121 (bottom), 147
Fielding Bowman: 30, 31
Mimi Findlay Antiques: 101 (top)
Robert Flack and Associates: 142
Ralph Gillis Architect: 18, 82, 83 (top), 106, 156
Peter Gisolf Associates: 32–33
Lil Groueff: 123
Mark Hampton: 138
Margaret Helfand Architects: 10
Hank Hubert: 154
In Design: 80–81
Kemp and Simmers By Design: 55 (top), 89
Killough-Irwin Design: 85

Leah Lenney: 100, 107, 141, 143, 144, 146, 148 (top and bottom)
Patterson, Flynn & Martin, Inc: 13 (top right)
Peter Marino Architect: 61
McMillen: 127
Peter McNamara: 108
Miller and Herriot: 50 (bottom)
Juan Mir A.S.I.D.: 72
Blue Mingers Architect/Barbara Shafer: 26, 40
Sandy Moore Artist: 34
Motif Designs: 38
Orr-Taylor: 160
Carole Price: 95
Phillip Read: 78 (right), 88
Scruggs and Myers: 77
Anne Tarasoff: 118
Julie Traratrola, Fabric by Boussac of France: 96
Jim Trunzo: 28, 114
David Williams Architect: 45, 50 (top), 53, 137
Chuck Winslow: 130 (top)
Stuart Wrede: 34, 73, 110
Gary Zarr: 74, 75
Tony Zunino Architect: 83 (bottom)
And with thanks to Charles Patteson Associates